Twayne's English Authors Series

Sylvia E. Bowman, *Editor*
INDIANA UNIVERSITY

Thomas Lodge

(TEAS) 59

Thomas Lodge

By WESLEY D. RAE

Utica College of Syracuse University

Twayne Publishers, Inc.   ::   New York

To Bette

Preface

THE achievements of Thomas Lodge (1558–1625) have not been adequately noted. Many readers know him as the author of the prose romance, *Rosalynde,* which William Shakespeare used as a basis for *As You Like It;* but too few readers know him as an excellent writer of Elizabethan lyrics; as a dramatist, critic, pamphleteer; as a sea adventurer in the Old and New World; as translator of great Classics; and lastly, as a dedicated physician in a London ravaged by the great plagues. A man of such outstanding and diverse talents—a truly Renaissance gentleman—deserves the attention of the serious reader.

Part of this neglect of Lodge's life and works results from the difficulty of obtaining his writings, which remained obscure until the late nineteenth century, when Sir Edmund Gosse reprinted the works, excluding the translations, for the Hunterian Society in a rapidly disappearing limited edition. Fortunately, Gosse's issue was in turn published in 1963; but the four hundred copies will not place the writings in the hands of many readers.

In the early 1930's several biographies of Lodge appeared. The first of these was N. B. Paradise's *Thomas Lodge,* followed by Charles Sisson's *Thomas Lodge,* Alice Walker's studies in the *Review of English Studies,* and E. A. Tenney's *Thomas Lodge.* In 1940, Samuel A. Tannenbaum published a bibliography of Lodge works and studies; and Pat Ryan, Jr., wrote in 1958 *Thomas Lodge Gentleman.* A full-length critical appraisal of the works has been lacking. The intention of this study is to bring some new light to the dark and disparate corners of Lodge's life, particularly his achievements as a writer, but with attention to his other accomplishments as well.

I received valuable assistance from the Huntington Library,

the Folger Shakespeare Library, the Bodleian Library, and the British Museum for microfilm copies of Lodge's works. I relied on the resources of the Hamilton College Library, and a special note of appreciation goes to Mary Dudley of the Utica College Library, who patiently helped me obtain the materials I needed. I am indebted to Mrs. Dorothy Sickels for reading the manuscript, and to Mrs. Grace Dempsey for typing.

WESLEY D. RAE

Utica College of Syracuse University

Contents

Chronology

1558   Birth of Thomas Lodge in London.

1564?   Page to the Stanleys, Earls of Derby.

1571   Enrolled in the Merchant-Taylors' School.

1573?   Trinity College, Oxford.

1578   Bachelor of Arts; admitted to Lincoln's Inn.

1579   *Reply to Gosson*, answering Stephen Gosson's *School of Abuse.*

1584   *Alarum against Usurers,* including the prose romance *Forbonius and Prisceria;* a verse satire, *Truth's Complaint over England.*

1586?   A drama, *The Wounds of Civil War.*

1586–
1587   Voyage with Captain Clarke to the Canaries and Azores.

1587?   *A Looking Glasse, for London and England,* a drama in collaboration with Greene.

1589   *Scillaes Metamorphosis,* including *The Discontented Satyr* and *Poems and Sonnets.*

1590   *Rosalynde: Euphues Golden Legacie.*

1591   *The Famous, true, and historicall life of Robert second Duke of Normandy;* and *Catharos, Diogenes in his Singularitie;* voyage around the world with Sir Thomas Cavendish.

1592   *Euphues Shadow, the Battaile of the Sences,* left with Robert Greene, and published while Lodge was with Cavendish.

1593   Return from the sea voyage; *The Life and Death of William Longbeard;* and *Phillis: Honoured with Pastorall Sonnets, Elegies, and amorous delights.*

1594   *A Spiders Webbe.* No copy of this work is extant; the last known copy disappeared about 1764.

1595   *A Fig for Momus.*

1596   *A Margarite of America; The Diuel coniured; Prosopopeia; Wits Misery and the Worlds Madnesse.*

1597   Entered the University at Avignon to study medicine.

1598   Doctor of Medicine, University of Avignon.

1601   *The Flowers of Lodowicke of Granada,* translation from the Latin.

1602   *The Famous and Memorable Workes of Iosephus;* incorporated as Doctor of Medicine at Oxford.

1603   *Treatise of the Plague.*

1604   Marriage to Joan Aldred; refused license to practice medicine in London; left England to practice in Belgium.

1610   Admitted to Licentiate of the College of Physicians in London.

1614   *The Workes both Morall and Natural of Lucius Annaeus Seneca.*

1621   *A learned Summary upon the famous Poeme of William of Saluste Lord of Bartas;* collection of medical cures, *The Poore Mans Talentt,* first published by the Hunterian Club, 1881.

1625   September, died of the plague in London.

CHAPTER 1

The Critics' War

I Early Education

EVERY man tries to connect with his age; and Thomas Lodge, gentleman, was no exception. Through various avenues in the England of his era, Lodge wound his way to find the connection. Most readers know Lodge as a writer of lyrics and prose romances; few know the variety of his writings, the effects of his prose style, or the experiments in literary forms that he introduced to English letters. A man who helped usher in the Golden Age of Elizabethan literature, his name belongs with the more famous names of Spenser, Sidney, Marlowe, and Shakespeare. Nor do most readers know the variety of his life; although we are primarily interested in him as a writer, we must see the larger view of his struggle which led him, at the end of his career, to become Thomas Lodge, Doctor of Physic.

Elizabeth I had come to the throne in 1558, the year most scholars accept as the date of Lodge's birth. Sir Thomas Lodge, his father, had been born in the year Henry VIII took the crown, 1509. For an age which believed in auspicious signs, these fortunate occurrences must have made the Lodges particularly optimistic; and Sir Thomas must have felt himself blessed. He experienced success after success: he took for his third wife Anne Loddington Lodge, a wealthy young widow who had inherited landed estates. Sir Thomas also had good fortune in his association with the Grocers' Company and the Muscovy Company; in his position as city alderman; and finally, as Lord Mayor of London in 1562, the year he was knighted.

These auspicious signs in the father's career were reflected early in his son's life. Thomas Lodge spent his youth in the household of the Stanleys, Earls of Derby. From 1564 to about

1571 he was a page to Henry Stanley, fourth Earl, and to his son, William Stanley. In this great house among famous people, Lodge must have learned music, languages, and the skills which identify a gentleman. What his duties as page were, and how extensive was his education, no one knows. He always wrote fondly of his memories of the Stanleys and of those early years of his life.

The second phase of his education began at the famous Merchant Taylors' School in London where he was enrolled as the son of a poor man at reduced tuition. In 1571 Sir Thomas had ended a term in prison for his debts, but he was surrounded with creditors who were to make life difficult for him until his death. Whatever the financial situation, Lodge spent two successful years at the school before entering Trinity College, Oxford, in 1573. There he had the good fortune to study with Sir Edward Hoby, a dynamic young man two years Lodge's junior who had taken his degree after only eight terms and who was destined to become a leading scholar and diplomat at Elizabeth's court. After four years of this exciting and stimulating atmosphere, Lodge took his degree in March, 1577-78. He was now ready to go to London, where he was admitted to the Inns of Court, the famous law schools, as a member of the society of Lincoln's Inn. There he would begin study for a legal career, an excellent springboard for service in the government or with a great nobleman.

II *London and Lincoln's Inn*

When Lodge took up residence in Lincoln's Inn, he was twenty years old, and undoubtedly he had that look of bright optimism which marks hundreds of young men just out of a university. He also must have carried some undergraduate manuscripts, for Elizabethan gentlemen considered writing a fashionable avocation, especially as the Golden Age of English literature was just beginning. At the Inns of Court, Lodge was in the midst of much of the budding literary energy: such early writers as George Turberville were members of the law society, and Thomas Sackville and Thomas Norton's *The Tragedy of Gorboduc* was performed by members of the Inner Temple for Queen Elizabeth.

April, 1578, and some of the months of 1579 must have been exciting for young Thomas. His older brother, William, was also a member of Lincoln's Inn; and Thomas as yet had no falling out with him or with the rest of his family. We can assume that he was on a reasonably comfortable allowance, surrounded by friends from Oxford, and slightly intoxicated at being a law student in the great city. But his good fortune did not last; when his mother died in 1579, she left Thomas in a predicament which, though she was well intentioned, made the best of his young years miserable. Thomas was her favorite son; and, though she did not approve of his leanings toward a literary career and, worse, those toward the Roman Catholic faith, she favored him over her other sons in her will. Thomas was to receive a landed estate, but not without encumbrances.[1] His brother William and Sir William Cordell, who were to act as executors of the will under bond, were to convey the estate to Thomas at age twenty-five. A careful woman, Lady Lodge added a codicil two days after she had signed the will, changing the estate to substitute certain properties which may have been designed to keep her son both a law student and a Protestant by withholding any ready money until he was, in her opinion, more mature.

Lady Lodge's reasons for changing the will may have been religious or economic, or both; we do not know exactly what prompted her actions, but it could not have been a secret from the Lodges that Thomas was writing and presumably neglecting the study of law. William no doubt reported to Sir Thomas and Lady Lodge what the boy was doing. It is quite certain that in 1578–79 he was busy writing pamphlets which allied him not only with writers, but with theater people. The effects of this year's activity and those activities up to 1585 were to have major influence on the many vicissitudes of Thomas' life.

While his son's star was rising somewhat shakily, Sir Thomas' star fell. As early as 1563 he was bankrupt due to the plagues, the wars with France, and his own over-extended speculation. But despite his financial difficulties, he must have noted young Thomas' adventures in London, and he shared Lady Lodge's fears. For, when he died in 1584, his intentions toward his son were quite clear: Thomas was disinherited. It may be that the father considered the property Lady Lodge had left him to be sufficient, but the slight was hard to ignore. Indeed, Sir Thomas and Sir William Cordell considered Thomas' life impossibly degenerate.[2] Ironically, young Thomas had the same penchant for mismanaging money that his father had.

The two men were much alike. Sir Thomas' life emphasizes the desire for expansion in all areas, a characteristic of many Englishmen in the reigns of the early Tudors. The spirit of noble independence inspired by such international figures as Cardinal Wolsey, Henry VIII, John Colet, Hugo Grocyn, and Sir Thomas More spurred adventure in many Englishmen. The younger Lodge felt the same desires, but they were elevated by his education and the changing times. The gentlemen of the 1560's had produced the genteel sons of the 1580's.

III   Morals and Methods in Writing

As a genteel son at Lincoln's Inn, Lodge began his avocation as a writer in a literary quarrel. But, before discussing Lodge's first work, we must consider the religious forces and Elizabethan methods in writing which influenced him. In the 1570's, the Puritan interests in England began attacks upon traditional entertainments, especially the theater. But the label *Puritan* is misleading since it is as difficult to sort out and define a Puritan in this era as it is to characterize an Existentialist in ours. Literary historians and critics use the term indiscriminately, but modern studies of Puritanism in literature that have grown out of Milton scholarship have shown the necessity for care in reaching a definition. We forget, for instance, that the Puritan movement under Queen Elizabeth was a reform wholly within the Established Church and was not the militantly organized movement against it that it became in the early years of the seventeenth century. In the earlier period Roman Catholics, English Catholics, and Puritans were all within the framework of one church; it becomes, therefore, almost impossible to attach the Puritan label to any except a few outstanding men.

But we can ascertain the fact that almost everyone who attached himself to the Puritan movement in any fashion decried plays and playwrights.[3] This characteristic was also shared by the Anglicans who supported the Puritan reformers in attacks on the stage. Archbishop Laud and Giles Fletcher, as representatives of the Anglican attitude, found nothing good to say about plays. In general, Anglican attacks were little different from the Puritan ones.[4] And, in summation, it may be said not only that this front against the theater was part of the concentrated attention upon public morality, but that concern with church organization and practices was a later development that makes distinctions within the church clearer.

Second, method in writing concerns what we consider to be plagiarism but what the Elizabethans called *imitation.* For example, Lodge borrowed much material for his works from Continental writers, and no less a figure than Shakespeare, as we have seen, based a play upon a later work of Lodge, to cite only two examples.

There are reasonable explanations which help us to understand this practice during this period. First, Aristotle's doctrine of imitation was widely accepted in the universities. Imitation denied independent invention in writing, and claimed all literary production as common property. These were primary laws; differences occurred only in interpretation by the individual writer. Pietro Bembo and Julius Caesar Scaliger among Continental critics, for instance, held for close imitation of Cicero in prose and of Virgil in poetry; others were more liberal, as was Baldassare Castiglione, whose views were available to English readers in Sir Thomas Hoby's translation of *The Book of the Courtier.* But all critics agreed that imitation was essential, that independent invention was bad practice, and that all written material was available for others' use. Once these facts are recognized, the modern reader better understands the Elizabethan imitator.

A specific example of imitation as the Elizabethans understood it is the following excerpt from Lodge's first work, the *Reply to Gosson.* William Ringler has found that Lodge relied heavily on a Continental source, Badius Ascensius' preface to an edition of Terence's plays (1502);[5] and Lodge did borrow extensively from this source, but he mentions his authority prominently: "Persius was made a poete *Diuino furore percitus;* and whereas the poets were sayde to call for the Muses helpe, ther mening was no other, as Iodocus Badius reporteth, but to call for heauenly inspiration from aboue to direct theyr endeauors." [6]

And then he continued: "that thys is trewe the name of Tragedye doth importe, for if you consider whence it came, you shall perceive (as Iodocus Badius reporteth) that it drewe his original of *Tragos, Hircus et Ode, Cantus* (so called), for that the actors thereof had in rewarde for theyr labour a gotes skynne fylled wyth wyne." [7] And: "Also Iodocus Badius will assertain you that the actors for shewing pleasure receued some profite." [8] Lodge gave more credit, for those who need to find credits, than ever a Shakespeare gave Lodge for *As You Like It*.

A second explanation for widespread imitation lies in the demand for books in the sudden burst of literary activity following 1580. The invention of the printing press signaled the end of one of the blackest periods of English letters; following the death of Chaucer the whole field was begun anew in the late fifteenth century when the first light of the Continental Renaissance reached England. Writing in a new language for a new age was a bright, fresh thing; and certainly writers had not had enough time or sound enough bases on which to establish a code of ethics. Too often we are ready to judge the writers of this period by our own standards, surrounded as we are by decades of copyright laws and other protections which the Elizabethans could hardly know. Universities were not yet preaching "give credit where credit is due," and the complicated day of the footnote had not yet appeared. Without this firmly established legal and ethical system, the Elizabethan writer should not be condemned by us without first placing ourselves in his frame of reference.

IV *The Literary Quarrel*

One of the amazing things about the literary quarrel over the stage and other entertainments is that it began so early. Elizabethan drama had certainly not yet emerged from university interludes and Italian comedies, and in 1579 *Everyman* was still the best play written in English. But, in spite of this scarcity, the temperature of the Elizabethan theater was dividing rapidly into two ranges, both rising; one was generated by the opposition—the Puritans—and the other was supported not only by new enterprisers, such as Richard Burbage, who saw profit in Elizabethan love of spectacle, but also by playwrights, who saw fame, or at least sustenance, in this same penchant.

There was evidently enough early activity on the stage and in literary production, however, to arouse comment; and such criticism began with John Northbrooke's pamphlet, *Treatise wherein Dicing, Dancing, Vain Plays or Interludes, with Other Idle Pastimes. . . . Are Reproved* (1577), a dialogue between unstable Youth and wise Age which relies on the pagan and Christian past for its argument against frivolous entertainments. Northbrooke mentions by name the two public playhouses just opened, the Theater and the Curtain, as evidence that Englishmen were turning away from sermons and the sterner stuff that had made them great in the past.

The next attack is a famous one, Stephen Gosson's *School of Abuse* (1579), to be considered later, which was followed by a tract ascribed to Anthony Munday, *A Second and Third Blast of Retreat* [retreat] *from Plays and Theaters* (1580), which like Northbrooke's work, condemns the congregating of persons, especially on Sunday, for any purpose other than worship. Of these two works, Gosson's *School of Abuse* deserves fuller attention since it prompted Lodge to prepare the first formal defense of plays, poetry, and entertainment in general.[9] In order to understand Lodge's position, we must first look at Gosson and his tract; for the argument between them was as personal as it was critical of contemporary entertainments in London.

Stephen Gosson was a man of generally unsavory fame who was Lodge's contemporary at Oxford, although there is no evidence that they were acquainted. He wrote plays in London, then turned against plays and playwrights as a vehement spokesman for the Puritans, and he ended his career as an Anglican clergyman who was a militant opponent of the Puritan cause. William Ringler, who has written a study attempting to rescue Gosson from critics' wrath at these sudden turns, states that Gosson was probably hired by Puritan interests to attack the stage.[10]

Gosson's *School of Abuse* is divided into two main parts, the historical and the moral evidence against plays and similar entertainments. For the historical argument, Gosson turned to the Greek and Roman writers for assistance. Ringler has shown how much Gosson depended on Plutarch, Dio Cassius, and others; but Plato was foremost because of his famous condemnation of poets which gave attackers so much pleasure and the apologists so much pain. Gosson lists the many ancients who banished poets, concluding that Homer is worth reading, but few others.

The moral argument of the *School* is more contemporary than the historical argument. Little condemnation of individual plays is found; his attack is directed much more against what goes on in the audience than against what is projected from the stage: "In our assemblies at playes in London, you shall see such heaving and shooving, suche ytching and shouldering to sytte by women. . . ." [11] He blames the theater, therefore, for being a market place for vice: "Every wanton and [his] paramour, everye man and his mistresse, every John and his Joane, every knave and his queane are there first acquainted, and cheapen the marchandise in that place, which they pay for else where, as they can agree." [12]

Gosson, who admits that some plays are worthy, names a few, and among them is one that represents "the greedinesse of worldly chusers, and the bloody minds of usurers," and his own play, *Catiline's Conspiracies*, which, as he says, is "usually brought in at the Theater," and which he acknowledges as "a pig of mine owne Sowe." [13] But he does not give us specific information about what he finds wrong with individual plays or with the whole of drama on the stage. The pamphlet concludes with a general condemnation of social London and with an appeal for Englishmen to "marke what wee were before, and what we are now." Englishmen were "in valure not yielding to Sythia; the women in courage passing the Amazons." But, he warns, "the exercise that is nowe among us is banquetting, playing, pyping, and dauncing, and all such delightes as may winne us to pleasure, or rocke us in sleepe." [14]

Gosson dedicated his work, without permission, to Sir Philip Sidney; and in a great show of moral bravado he addressed one of two letters to Sir Richard Pipe, Lord Mayor of London, to advise him that, "If your Honour desire to see the Citie well governed, you must as well set to your hand to thrust out abuses, as showe your selfe willing to have all amended." [15] The other letter was to "the Gentlewomen, Citizens of London," asking them to amend their conduct:

You must keepe your sweete faces from scorching in the sun, chapping in the winde, and warping in the weather, which is best perfourmed by staying within; and if you perceive your selves in any daunger at your owne doors, either allured by curtesie in the day, or assaulted with musike in the night, close uppe your eyes, stoppe your eares, tye up your tongues: when they speake, answeare not; when they hallowe, stoope not. . . . These are hard lessons which I teach you: neverthelesse, drinke uppe the potion, though it like not your tast, and you shal be eased: resist not the surgeon, though hee strike with his knife, and you shall bee cured.[16]

Although Gosson goes far afield in his attack and although the pamphlet is short, scarcely any activity is left untouched; and we cannot miss the arrogance of the self-assured university student in his first moral endeavor.

The *School of Abuse* must have created quite a stir among the law students of the Inns of Court, who, as we have seen, were supporters of the new theater; indeed, Gray's Inn had as a member George Gascoigne, whose plays had already met some popularity on the stage. Gascoigne and others no doubt encouraged the young Lodge to try his hand in a defense of their position, and the result was the *Reply to Gosson*. The *Reply* was published privately, without license from the London authorities, and was almost immediately withdrawn from circulation, apparently by Puritan city officials. Few readers saw the work, and it may well have been that Gosson never read it. Only two copies survive, and they are badly printed.[17]

Other men had preceded Lodge in writing about poetry, such as Roger Ascham's chapter in the *Scholemaster* (1570), Richard Willes' Latin *Poetatum Liber* (1573), George Gascoigne's *Certaine Notes of Instruction* (1575), and George Whetstone's brief note in the *Dedication* to *The Right excellent and famous Historye of Promos and Cassandra* (1578); but none of these authors was required to defend creative activity in any area. Although not much of Lodge's defense is original, it is stated in English for Englishmen to read.

Lodge begins his argument with a general defense of poets and poetry; then he discusses specifically music, plays, and, though briefly, "Carders, Dicers, Fencers, Bowlers, Daunsers, and Tomblers." In reply to Gosson's contention that fictional or creative poetry is vain in comparison with history and philosophy, Lodge asks: "If you say that Poetes did labour about nothing, tell me (I besech you) what wonders wroughte those your dunce Doctors in ther reasons *de ente, et non ente*, in theyr definition of no force, and les witt?" [18] And, as Lodge pursues Gosson, he asks more pointed questions: "What made Erasmus labor in Euripides tragedies? Did he indeauour by painting them out of Greke into Latin to manifest sinne vnto vs?" [19] Or he asks: "You looke vpon the refuse of the abuse, nether respecting the importance of the matter nor the weighte of the wryter. . . . Chaucer in pleasant vein can rebuke sin vncontrold: and though he be lauish in the letter, his sence is serious." [20]

In referring to Classical examples of the poet's "fury," through the well-known stories, especially of Hesiod and Persius, Lodge precedes Sidney's statement in the *Defense of Poetry* about the divine nature of poetry: "I reson not that al poets are holy, but I affirme that poetry is a heauenly gift, a perfit gift, then which I know not greater pleasure." [21] And finally Lodge admits that some poets and playwrights, as Gosson had charged, write scandalous poetry and plays: "I abore those poets that sauor of ribaldry: I will with the zealous admit the expullcion of such enormities: poetry is dispraised not for the folly that is in it, but for the abuse whiche manye ill wryters couller by it." [22]

Little of real critical value emerges from Lodge's *Reply* or from Gosson's *School of Abuse*. But we should not expect to find sound criticism when so little had been produced to nourish it. Not until the age of John Dryden was there a sufficient heritage in literature upon which to build solid critical foundations.

V *Euphuistic Style*

Aside from content, the style of the *Reply* deserves some comment, for it is the style that Lodge uses in all of his later prose. This style had its progenitor in John Lyly, who was supposedly a friend of Gosson's, and who was a contemporary of both Gosson and Lodge at Oxford. Lyly's *Euphues* (1578) brought to English literature a style so distinctive that it is called *euphuistic*. Briefly, it involves the use of elaborately balanced phraseology, loaded with illustrations from the commonplaces of life, or from the fantastic speculations of unnatural natural history. Gosson's *School of Abuse* is heavily euphuistic throughout: "I must confesse that poets are whetstones of wit, notwithstanding that wit is dearely bought: where honie and gall are mixt, it will be hard to sever the one from the other. The deceitfull phisition geveth sweete syrroppes to make his poyson goe downe the smoother: the jugler casteth a myst to work the closer: the syrens songue is the saylers wracke; and fowlers whistle the birdes death; the wholesome baite the fishes bane." [23] The alliteration in the first sentence is followed by examples that are neatly balanced but seemingly interminable to the modern reader. The pace is leisurely, and the symmetry is carefully worked out by the writer.

Lodge's *Reply* is somewhat more sparing of these characteristics; he preserves in all of his prose works what is best in Lyly—the balance, alliteration, and parallelism: "Protogenes can know Appelles by his line though he se him not, and wise men can consider by the Penn the aucthoritie of the writer thoughe they know him not. The Rubie is discerned by his pale rednes; and who hath not hard that the Lyon is knowne by hys clawes? Though Æsopes craftie crowe be never so deftlye decked, yet is his double dealing esely desiphered." [24] The parallel structure in the "though . . . though" clauses of the first sentence do not intrude heavily on the reader's senses, and the three illustrations or applications are not stated in the same tiresome iteration that marks the worst of Lyly's prose and that of most of his imitators.

VI *The Results*

Content and style should have made the *Reply* reasonably successful; but it could not circulate freely, as we have seen. It had, however, made an impression in a way Lodge probably never considered: to his own later sorrow, he had made a large part of his defense a personal attack on Gosson. In the second paragraph of the *Reply*, Lodge begins the abuse and sets the tone for what later would become a full symphony: "There came to my hands lately a litle (woulde God a wittye) pamphelet, baring a fayre face as though it were the scoole of abuse; but, being by me aduisedly wayed, I fynd it the oftscome of imperfections, the writer fuller of wordes then iudgement, the matter certainly as ridiculus as serius." [25]

Throughout the pamphlet, Lodge keeps the personal fight close to the surface, even though it appears he never so much as met Gosson. Gosson has a "giddy brain"; is compared to Terence's Gnatho, "Whom if we shoulde seeke in our dayes, I suppose he would not be farr from your parson." Lodge accuses Gosson of using "diuinite to couer your knauery," and tells him, "Alas! Simple Irus, begg at knowledge gate awhile." Even when Lodge makes a good point for the defense of poetry, he cannot resist a stab at his opponent, as when he describes the divine inspiration of the poet—the poetic fury—and concludes with "it pitieth me to bring a rodd of your owne making to beate you wythal." [26] This personal invective must have stung Gosson, although he might have expected it; in any case, he later settled accounts.

The restless, stung spirit of the indefatigable Gosson did not allow him to remain silent after the personal jabs Lodge wrote in his *Reply*. Indeed, before Lodge's work was suppressed at the printer's, Gosson had heard a rumor the *Reply* was in process and had hurried to write *A Short Apology for the School of Abuse*, which was prabably printed in November, 1579.[27] The first part of the treatise is a reply to the now lost *Straunge News out of Affrick* by an unknown author, which Gosson mentions pointedly in the beginning of his *Ephemerides of Phialo;* the last few paragraphs are centered on

Lodge's *Reply*, of which Gosson has only heard reports but apparently not the name of the writer: "Our players since I set out the *Schole of Abuse*, haue trauailed to some of mine acquaintance of both Vniuersities, with fayre profers, and greater promises of rewardes, yf they woulde take so much paine as too write against mee." [28]

Although Gosson does not know Lodge personally, he is ready to hurl personal abuse: "they were driuen to flie to a weake hedge, and fight for themselues with a rotten stake. . . . It is told mee that they haue got one in London to write certain *Honest excuses*, for so they tearme it, to their dishonest abuses which I reuealed." [29] And Gosson then promises, once the writer and his work are known, a great battle; but he had to wait for some time to get a copy of Lodge's *Reply*. By 1582 he had probably seen it, but he had also been needled by the now lost *Play of Playes*, another defense by an unknown writer, both of which Gosson attacked in *Playes Confuted in Five Actions* (1582).[30] He had dedicated the *School of Abuse* and the *Ephemerides of Phialo* (1579) to Sir Philip Sidney without response; he now dedicated his new work to Sir Frances Walsingham, bulwark of Puritanism. From the beginning Lodge is dealt with roundly, as Gosson addresses Walsingham: "I thoughte it necessarye to nettle one of their Orators aboue the rest, not of any set purpose to deface hym, because hee hath dealt very grossely, homely, and vncharitably with me, but like a good Surgeon to cut, and to seare, when the place requireth, for his own amendment." [31] And cut and sear he does, for he says that Lodge ". . . is (as I heare by hys owne frendes, to hys repentance if he can perceiue it) hunted by the heauy hand of God, and because little better than a vagarant. . . ." [32] In the first action he calls Lodge "in witt, simple; in learning, ignorant; in attempt, rash; in name, Lodge. . . ." [33] But Gosson did not really know his opponent; he calls him William Lodge.[34]

The quarrel, now largely personal in one aspect, and widely varying in another—Gosson insists on arguing on moral grounds, Lodge on esthetic—was not settled until 1584 when Lodge ended it in the preface to *Alarum Against Usurers.*

From that point both writers dropped their weapons, and were not heard of again in the ensuing critical exchanges. Sir Philip Sidney's *A Defense of Poetry*, written in the 1580's but not published until 1595, became the greatest defense of poetry and drama that the age produced. This urbane and witty pamphlet, written in a style stripped of euphuistic excess, and so orderly in its presentation, must have made it clear to Gosson, Lodge, and others that it was useless for them to continue the battle.

VII   *"A Doleful Dump"*

What interests us at this point is the "heauy hand of God." As we have seen, Lodge had come to London in 1578, had settled into the life of the Inns easily, and within a year had mingled in the pamphlet war. Three years later he had entered his supplication for the Master of Arts degree at Oxford, and it had been accepted.[35] Some time between February, 1581, the date of Lodge's petition, and 1582, the date of Gosson's *Plays Confuted*, the heavy hand descended: Lodge did not receive his degree. This fact, together with notices in the Acts of the Privy Council, help fill in the lack of known data during these years. The first notice in the Acts is on June 27, 1581. A Thomas Lodge[36] was called to Council to answer certain charges—what they were is not known—and he was imprisoned until autumn of that year. Edward A. Tenney believes imprisonment arose from Thomas' turn to the Roman faith.[37]

The fact is that Lodge was imprisoned for many months. We know he had become a member of the Roman Church, but the date is impossible to determine, and it is unlikely the conversion got much publicity in Elizabethan England. Since his lawsuits with moneylenders and family did not begin for several years, the imprisonment seems, therefore, to point to recusancy, which would not be an unusual charge during Elizabeth's reign.

The reasoning behind Lodge's turn in faith is clearer. Sir Thomas Lodge, sometime dapper Lord Mayor of London, had dabbled freely in various religions. Born in the year of Henry VIII's accession, he had lived and flourished under both Edward VI and Mary Tudor; so young Thomas would have had some acquaintance with the "old religion" through his father, and perhaps through other members of his family. Not only had he found Roman influence at Oxford, but there were a number of recusants at Lincoln's Inn. It is not unlikely that the cloak-and-dagger atmosphere of the outlawed church appealed to young Lodge—if the tenets of faith did not.

While in prison, Lodge revised the work of author-soldier Barnabe Rich, *The Strange and Wonderful Adventures of Don Simonides*. In Lodge's dedicatory verses he complains that his "long distresse hath laied his Muse to rest, / Or duld his Sprightes, or sences at the lest." The final stanza appends a moral which may indicate his own feelings:

> I leaue thee now, my Muse affordes no more,
> A doleful dumpe, pulles backe my pleasant vaine,
> Looke thou for praise, by men of learned lore,
> Despise the skoffe, that growes from shuttle braine,
> For me I honour thee for taking paine,
> And wishe eche youth, that spendes his tyme amisse,
> Would fixe his penne to write such woorkes as this.[38]

As soon as he was released from prison, Lodge was greeted by Gosson's *Plays Confuted*, as we have seen. Not only was he attacked personally, but attacked in his home court; for Gosson addressed a letter prefacing the work "to the Right Worshipful Gentlemen and students, of both Universities, and the Inns of Court." Lodge's brother William was a member of the Inns; it must have been somewhat embarrassing for the enthusiastic young writer to return from prison only to find his reputation at stake.

But literary problems were the least of Lodge's immediate worries. In 1582–83 there began a long series of family-founded financial difficulties. His family undoubtedly disapproved of his writing pamphlets, his consorting with Papist beliefs, his failure to achieve the master's degree, and his imprisonment. The Lodges were becoming landed aristocrats in the second generation; to them, son Thomas was a failure.

At his father's funeral in 1584, Thomas must have been a disappointed but thoughtful young man. He certainly was no success as a writer, and prospects of civil appointment after imprisonment were slight. He had been attacked personally in print; he was disinherited and rejected by his family. Thomas Lodge must have decided it was time for him to take a new direction.

CHAPTER 2

Writer and Privateer

I An Alarum Against Usurers

LODGE tired of the literary controversy that had gotten out of control; moreover, no future as a writer could develop from an endless, profitless quarrel. He finally ended it in a dignified manner in the preface to his new work, which included some of the first literary pieces that we know of. The little volume published in 1584 as *An Alarum Against Usurers* also contained the *History of Forbonius and Prisceria* and a long poem, *Truth's Complaint over England*. These works are either bits he had put together as a student at Oxford, or his efforts at Lincoln's Inn to begin his career as a writer; but with certainty the *Alarum* was composed in London. All of the pieces are moral in tone: the *Alarum* is the nearest thing to a sermon Lodge ever wrote, and the *Complaint* is morally redolent of the Medieval *Piers Plowman*. The moral content was doubtless Lodge's attempt to restore his reputation.

Two factors contributed to Lodge's knowledge of usurers which he used in the *Alarum:* first, his family had disinherited him; and, if he had an allowance, it was not sufficient to allow him to live as he desired. Secondly, he was forced to turn to the only other source he knew, the London moneylenders. Dates are uncertain, but the evidence shows that Lodge was heavily indebted to moneylenders by 1584.[1] The *Alarum* is a record of his bitter experiences in the form of an elaborate warning to young men to stay out of the clutches of unscrupulous merchant-usurers. Lodge should have had ample warning himself since one of his father's apprentices, George Stoddard, had risen by devious means through moneylending to become a wealthy, respected London citizen.[2]

The *Alarum* is a humble, dignified confession. It has been suggested, and I think rightly, that the *Alarum* was intended primarily for Old Sir Thomas and Sir William Cordell; but it came too late to be much more than a personal vindication.[3] Lodge was, however, more successful in the prefatory epistle with his termination of the quarrel with Gosson. The work is, first of all, dedicated to Sir Philip Sidney—with permission— whom Gosson had twice tried to attract without success. Lodge then addresses an epistle to "the Gentlemen of the Inns of Court" in which he answers Gosson's address to Lodge's fellow law students in statements that are noble and brief. Gosson has argued, he says, *a persona,* but it is unjust to "conclude without occasion": "But thy base degree, subiect to seruile attempts, measureth all things according to cauelling capacitie, thinking because nature hath bestowed upon thee a plausible discourse, thou maist in thy sweet termes present the sowrest and falsest reports you canst imagine." [4]

Although Lodge himself had begun the *a persona* attack, he does dispose rather neatly of Gosson and his "plausible discourse." The brief and proud conclusion states that Gosson, "not measuring me by my birth, but by the subiect I handled . . . upbraided me in person, when he had no quarrell. . . ." He sees no further use in replying, and he accuses Gosson of playing "bo peep." Lodge likens himself to Philip of Macedon and Gosson to Nicanor when Philip rewarded Nicanor's abuse with courtesy; so Lodge says of Gosson: "now in publicke I confesse thou hast a good pen, and if thou keepe thy Methode in discourse, and leaue thy slandering without cause, there is no doubt but thou shalt be commended for thy coppie, and praised for thy stile." [5] Lodge then justifies himself to his fellow Innsmen for the reports of the "heauy hand of God" and for slanderous gossip about his behavior and companions: "so now you will not cease to be friendly, both in protecting of this iust cause, from uniust slander, and my person from that reproch, which, about two yeares since, an iniurious cauiller obiected against me. . . ." [6]

Barnabe Rich, who dedicated some verses to Lodge's *Alarum,* gave at least one man's confidence in Lodge during the controversy, with a pun on Gosson: "That both the subiect and thy stile is good / Thou needs not feare the scoffe of Momus' brood," and "If thus it be, good Lodge continue still, / Thou

needst not feare Goose sonne or Ganders hisse." [7] Thus ended
the pamphlet war. No more is heard on this score from either
Gosson or Lodge; others directed the fight leading to the closing of the theaters in 1642.

The epistle shows us a sober, much less glib young man.
There is a certain bounce and offensive attack in the *Reply*
which has been smoothed down to an even-paced, more subtle
approach. Much of the wide-eyed optimism of the university
man of five years ago is gone. Once Gosson is disposed of, the
main subject appears. In the dedication to Sidney, Lodge vows
to describe the "image of a licentious Vsurer, and the collusions
of diuelish incroachers. . . ." In the epistle to the gentlemen of
the Inns of Court, he states in somewhat stronger language: "I
haue published heere of set purpose a tried experience of
worldly abuses, describing heerein not only those monsters
which were banished Athens, I meane Vsurers, but also such
deuouring caterpillers, who not only have fatted their fingers
with many rich forfaitures, but also spread their venim among
some priuate Gentlemen of your profession. . . ." [8]

Two points of some importance are present. First, Lodge
writes "of set purpose," and the emphasis indicates there is
more than mere literary recognition implied in writing the
pamphlet. It is not unreasonable to assume that Lodge may
have expected legal action against usurers from influential
members of the Inns or from court since the concluding section
seems to indicate this motive. Secondly, when Lodge states that
usurers have "spread their venim among some priuate Gentlemen of your profession," he is clearly addressing a wider audience than the gentlemen of the Inns of Court. He may be say-
ing "I'm not the only one . . . ," but I think that he is setting
the moral tone. This is a genuine warning, almost a sermon, or
at least a lecture, to his fellows against the evil toils of moneylenders. Shakespeare's Shylock and Marlowe's *Jew of Malta*,
although set outside England, are nevertheless extreme cases
based on the usurious practices in England. We may also take
the example of Lodge himself, whose ample experience in
courts as a litigant in bond-making cases presents a clear picture of the young gentleman in London.[9]

The *Alarum* departs from Lodge's earlier pamphlet in several aspects. He quits the firmly accepted Renaissance principle of imitation—the work is his own invention; and he uses the euphuistic style introduced by Lyly much more freely than in the *Reply,* which is dated only a year later than *Euphues.* By 1583 or 1584 the style became generally popular, and the balanced, alliterative, parallel sentences with their everlasting natural history similes appear in several places. The opening paragraph is an example of the remarkable departure from the style of the *Reply* and closer imitation of *Euphues:* "No maruell though the wise man accompted all things vnder the sun vain, since the cheefest creatures be mortall: and no wonder though the world rune at random, since iniquitie in these later dayes hath the vpper hand. The alteration of states if they be looked into, and the ouerthrow of houses, if they be but easely laid in open viewe, what eye would not shed teares to see things so transitorie; and what wisedome would not indeauour to dissolue the inconuenience." [10]

This is a good beginning because the balance, parallelism, and alliteration are assets in these sentences. Occasionally Lodge slips, however, into euphuistic excess: "But as among a tree of fruite there bee some withered fallings, and as among wholesome hearbes there growes some bitter *Colloquintida:* so it cannot be, but among such a number of Marchaunts, there shoulde bee some, that degenerate from the true name and nature of Marchaunts." [11] Even this style is moderate, and it is the one Lodge adapted for much of his prose. He took, as we have already noted in Chapter 1, the best of the popular style for his own, and left the more fantastic, monotonous constructions behind.

The moral tone is also different from Lodge's earlier work. The earnestness and serious dedication belies—or identifies— the young man about town who has been visited by the "heauy hand of God." If Lodge hoped the *Alarum* would placate his father and his financial guardian—merchants both—he stated his purpose carefully: "Of these men [degenerate Marchaunts] I write, and of none other, my inuectiue is priuate, I will not write generall." [12] The whole operation of the unscrupulous merchant is then cleverly detailed. He deals in "refuse commoditie," some almost worthless merchandise which prospective victims must turn into cash to realize their loans. Then there must be a middle man: "They finde oute . . . some olde soaking undermining Solicitour . . ." who is paid to find out inexperienced, impecunious young men haunting the region of St. Paul's Cathedral or elsewhere. Once found, they prey upon these "melancholy men," discontent because of lack of ready money.

Lodge uses dialogue to illustrate how the young man is snared, just as Lyly used dialogue in *Euphues*. But Lodge's speeches are swift, to-the-point, and not nearly so preachy as Lyly's. Under the silver-tongued solicitor's spell, the young man agrees to seek the wonders credit will hold out for him; and a bond is signed, whereby the young man is to take "commodity" from the generous merchant, sell it, and keep the profit as proceeds of the loan. A bond is signed for twenty pounds, the merchandise—worth perhaps at the best five pounds—is sold for only two pounds. But the twenty pounds, plus interest, must be repaid. The solicitor then guides the young man to a tailor, who is also part of the ring, and to Mistress Minx, who conveys favors of one sort or another. The rest of the story is familiar to readers of Luke 15: The son must go home to a forgiving father, who delivers a Polonius lecture to his son in euphuistic style.

On incontinence the father lectures at some length: "Incontinencie (young man) is the root of all inconuenience, it dulleth the memorie, decayeth the body, and perisheth the bones, it maketh stedfast fickle, beautifull deformed, and vertuous vicious. . . ." [13] The son listens and promises to reform, but at the first opportunity he returns to the Inns of Court and to Mistress Minx. In this second act, the man is deserted by all, disinherited by his father, and imprisoned. In prison he ruefully laments "it is better to haue the stripes of a friend, than the kisses of a flatterer." [14] His old pal the solicitor appears; gets him out of prison, the young man himself becomes an "olde soaking undermining Solicitour"; and the victim, now the villain, repeats the whole action on another unsuspecting young man.

The pamphlet ends with a strong plea for action to stop such fleecing. In traditional phrases Lodge rehearses past cases,

Classical and contemporary, in which usurers and usury were outlawed. He argues that the fall of one family begins another with the simple assertion that a usurious father can hardly found a good family, and begins to sound biblical:"What is it to get good, and to loose happinesse? to enioye much riches, and little rest? to haue many Lordships, and much hart-breake?" [15] To the argument that many usurers are good Christians, Lodge answers: "If they heare correction of sin by often haunting of sermons, yet continue their wickednesse, when they know what it worketh: their actions are wicked, their liues dissolute, their ends desperate." [16]

In prose indicating the sinews of Lodge's later great style, he begins the constructive conclusion: "A lamentable case it is, to see how true simplicitie, the maintainer of peace, is almost altogether exiled out our common weale: and that worldlye wit doeth wade so farre, as heauenlye wise are brought into admiration of their mischiefe." [17] The remedy Lodge then offers is legal—more controls, licensing, bonding. And wards, including sons, should be given more allowance to prevent their being forced into the hands of usurers. The parting lines are a curse, as from an Elizabethan Jeremiah, on such men: "Sathan whom you haue serued shall accuse you, the poor afflicted members of Christ shall beare witnesse against you, so that in this horror and confusion you shall desire the mountaines to fall vpon you, and the hils to couer you from the fearfull indignation of the Lord of hostes, and the dredfull condemnation of the Lambe Jesus." [18] But the fire and brimstone had little effect, at least upon Lodge himself. For many years to come he was plagued by incessant suits and countersuits with his creditors.

II Forbonius and Prisceria

Since Elizabethans loved variety, it was not unusual for a pamphlet to bear riders, as did the *Alarum* volume. *Forbonius and Prisceria* is an early attempt to capitalize on the success of Lyly's *Euphues* and on Robert Greene's romances, such as *Pandosto* and *Menaphon*, in the same style. How much Lodge depended on his predecessors and how much on invention is, however, difficult to ascertain. In the 1560's, beginning with William Painter's *Palace of Pleasure* (1566) and remaining popular through Barnabe Rich's *Don Simonides* (1581), the prose romance had a large following. Heliodorus' *Aethiopica* and the style of other Greek romances of the early Christian era came to the Elizabethans through Thomas Underdown's *An Ethiopian History,* and gave prose narrative the far-away aspect of forgotten lands, beautiful heroines, powerful heroes, and magicians—all woven into plots so intricate the reader reels at the developments.

The Italian *novelle* gave narrative its practical reality in character types, and the Greek romances lent the plots. One other ingredient was style, and, as we have seen, Lyly's *Euphues* supplied it. Although Lodge's romance imitates these earlier works, there is little of the Heliodorian complex plot which Sidney emulated in his *Arcadia* (1590). The result in Lodge's work—a brief, seldom motivated action that is characteristic of Elizabethan fiction—is a plot that follows the Romeo-Juliet form of feuding families and parted lovers. The gymnosophist Apollonius is like Friar Laurence: he hands out advice to Forbonius much as the Friar does to Romeo: "the greatest wisdome is to measure euery attempt with his casualties, and if ought happen that may seem impossible, to cast off the rayne, and suffer it to passe in that form it was concluded in." [19]

After the initial exposition of laments, what plot there is develops. The magic mirror of Apollonius would appeal to Elizabethan readers, and the exchange of letters by its means speeds the action. Prisceria's exile leads naturally to the pastoral setting, where, disguised as Arvalio the shepherd, Forbonius can address his mistress in poetry. The "sonnet" which Forbonius breathes to the woodland—the first lyric expression we know from Lodge's pen—contains in the last stanza some of the delicate lyricism which is still recognized as one of Lodge's best claims to fame:

> And if the aire by yeelding calme consent,
>   Make sweet Prisceria priuie to my suite,
> Vouchsafe deere sweet, that beautie may relent,
>   And graunt him grace, whom distance maketh mute:
> So either hope shall make me climbe the skie
> Or rude repulse enforce my fancies flie.[20]

The disguised Forbonius reveals himself to Prisceria after delivering her a long "Aeglog" in riming, ragged couplets of over two hundred lines; all are end stopped; and they do not reflect Lodge at his best, for only later in his career did he learn the technique of the polished couplet. The "Aeglog" relates a pastoral tale of Corinna and Corulus, shepherds both; and it has much of the spirit and substance which later emerged in the first successful Ovidian verse narrative in English literature: Lodge's *Scillaes Metamorphosis*. Corinna loves Corulus, but he spurns her, only to find himself smitten later. The machinations of the gods add to the tale; it lacks only the Ovidian background to make it in line with the later erotic poetry.

The conclusion of *Forbonius and Prisceria* is happy and moralistic. Lodge adds a riddling touch at the end borrowed from Chaucer's *Franklin's Tale* and from other talespinners:

Now Ladies and Gentlewomen, I must leaue this to your consideration, whether the louers for their constancie are more to be commended, or the olde man for his patience more to be wondered at: I leaue you to fit that conclusion till you haue read what is written, promising you that if my rude discourse haue wrought you anye pleasure, I will both labor heerafter to serue all occasions, and so fixe my studies as they shall not far differ from your fantasies: and thus crauing you to winke at an errour, and commend as the cause requireth, I take my leaue: willing to be made priuie if I haue anye wayes trauayled to your contentment.[21]

Lodge's prose style, as always, is certain. He knows just how much ornamentation to add. He is never dulling to exasperation, as Lyly is; he is never complex to frustration, as Greene sometimes is; instead we have passages of moderation: "Alasse (vnhappy Prisceria) what vntoward destinie hath befallen thee? That in thy flowing yeares and prime of beautie, thou art become a thrall to vncertaine pleasure. . . ." [22] The method of narration is much like *Euphues*, especially in the long discourses the leading characters hold with themselves as in Prisceria's lament: "Thou louest Forbonius, and why? for his vertue; yet thy father hateth him vpon olde grudges, with whom when rancour preuayleth, what may be more lookt for, then contempt and denyall? But Forbonius seeketh Prisceria's fauor, not Solduuius friendship: but Prisceria cannot enioy Forbonius, without Solduuius fauor. . . ." [23] The typical tête-à-tête with one's conscience—in the third person—leaves this method of character development far from the attempts that Lodge and others were soon to make.

There is some discouraging duplication in these speeches, especially in the early pages of the romance. Lodge may have been in a hurry to fill out the *Alarum* volume; there seems to be little other excuse for the repetition in these speeches against Fortune or Destiny. Prisceria's speech reads: "Alasse that in prefixing the torment, shee [Fortune] hath not proffered a remedye, or in bestowing an Vlcer, hath not vouchsafed a corrasiue." [24] And Forbonius almost echoes her words: "Alas you destinies, whose courses are ineuitable: how fortuneth it, that in bestowing casualties in mans life, you prescribe not meanes to preuent misfortunes? And onelye beginning to fester the heart, prefixe no presidents, whereby the humours may be expelled." [25]

Lodge hoped that the *Forbonius and Prisceria* would reach an appreciative audience; he dedicated the work, as Lyly did in the *Euphues,* to the "ladies and gentlewomen" he hoped would read the romance. He had no luck; *Forbonius and Prisceria* was printed once in 1584, and its first reprint in 1853 was by a male scholar, David Laing, for a largely male-scholar audience. N. B. Paradise succinctly judges the work: "The romance can no longer be read with much delight, but it marks an important step in the development of English prose fiction." [26] The important step includes, in summation, a more direct plot line than earlier attempts, a tempering of euphuistic style, and the inclusion of poetry with prose in the development of the story. *Forbonius and Prisceria* was a sapling; the tree would bear better fruit in Lodge's later works.

III   Truth's Complaint

The third contribution to the *Alarum* volume is *Truth's Complaint over England,* the first long poem Lodge published, the content and style of which look back rather than forward. Highly Medieval, it is reminiscent of the *Mirror for Magistrates* poetry, and especially of Thomas Sackville's "Induction," whose rime royal stanza it imitates. Sackville was the master of this kind of poetry, but Lodge may also have developed his style from works such as John Skelton's *Bowge of Court*.[27] The satiric tradition is that which began with *Piers Plowman* and Chaucer and that grew under Skelton, George Gascoigne, and Spenser until it was overshadowed by the revival of Classical satire with Lodge, John Donne, John Hall, and John Marston.

Complaint, a general term, applies to any poem in which the poet mourns his fate. In Lodge's poem the personification *Truth* mourns the fate of England; Chaucer, Sir Thomas Wyatt, Skelton, and others preceded Lodge in criticizing the erratic behavior of princes, courts, lawyers, and merchants. The goddess Truth pours out her sorrow to the poet who ". . . in fragrant field with woes opprest, / Gan walke to driue out melancholy griefe" [28] and who heard Truth lamenting by a river. She longs for the old time when all Englishmen were noble, an age now tarnished; but she is not ready to abandon all: "And yet I see not Sodom: some are good" (85). The worst are flatterers abroad in the land:

> Where craft dooth keepe true meaning in suspence;
> And wily worldlings couer their pretence
> With holy shapes, and in a holy coate,
> Dooth flattry praise those men that swim a floate.
> (ll. 158–61)

Truth finally departs the Island; she wishes to remain but is banished by the inhabitants: "And thus she said: You Ilanders adieu, / You banisht me, before I fled from you" (ll. 202–3).

The subject and form are quite different from the "Aeglog" of *Forbonius and Prisceria*, but we can see improvements even though it is possible that Lodge wrote *Truth's Complaint* during his university days. A stanza illustrates the worst and the best of Lodge's verse at this stage:

> For as the horse well mand abides the bit,
> And learnes his stop by raine in riders hand,
> Where mountaine colt that was not sadled yet,
> Runnes headlong on amidst the fallowed land,
> Whose fierce resist scarce bends with anie band:

So men reclaimde by vertue, tread aright,
Where led by follies, mischiefes on them light.
(ll. 71–77, p. 87)

The analogy, though apt, is stiff; the lines unbroken; but the
couplet rescues all and points to later poetry, some of which
ranks with the best produced by the Elizabethans.

The publication of the *Alarum* volume caused little alarm
among readers. It contained variety, and all three pieces were
certainly in vogue; but none enjoyed a second printing. Lodge's
first effort, the *Reply*, was forbidden; his second was merely
accepted. No one can doubt the bitterness Lodge was feeling.
He had been estranged from his family, ridiculed before his
fellows, and only tolerated in print. It was time to seek a new
avenue.

IV The Wounds of Civil War

The years 1585–88 pose difficult problems in recording
Lodge's life. After his only qualified success as a writer of pamphlets, romances, and poems, he turned to other activities: to
writing for the stage and to adventure on the sea. Which activity came first is a matter for debate. The facts are these: Lodge
wrote two plays, *The Wounds of Civil War* (c. 1586) and, in
collaboration with Robert Greene, *A Looking Glass for London
and England* (c. 1587). We also know he sailed with a Captain
John Clarke to the Canary Islands, during which time he wrote
Rosalynde. But authorities disagree on the dates of the plays
and of the voyage. N. B. Paradise maintains Lodge sailed as far
as the Canaries on Sir Walter Raleigh's 1585 voyage to Virginia,
and returned via another vessel. A John Clarke is listed by
Hakluyt as one of the "principal Gentlemen" on the voyage.[29]
Paradise then dates Lodge's return sometime before September, 1585, or April, 1586, when Lodge is mentioned as a witness
in a lawsuit.[30] E. A. Tenney finds evidence that Lodge sailed on
the *Gold Noble* on a later voyage with Clarke in November,
1586, and returned in 1587; for the *Gold Noble* fought against
the Spanish Armada in 1588.[31]

Both are conjectures, but Tenney's view is more likely since
it is surrounded by circumstantial evidence. Lodge mentions in

the preface to *Rosalynde* that he sailed "with Capt. Clarke"; if he had been a part of the Raleigh expedition, it seems likely he would have used that grand gentleman's name. In addition, it has been noted that, if Lodge returned in 1586, a lapse of four years ensues before he published the *Rosalynde*.[32] If he wrote it on board ship within a few months, he would not have held it four years for some unknown reason, for Lodge was not a polisher.

But until more concrete evidence appears, all possibilities must be considered, and none of the alternatives taken as positive. Out of the confusion, we do know one thing: Lodge made a sea voyage between 1585 and 1587. Disgraced second sons could bolster their fortunes on such adventures, and Lodge needed money. But he also needed some new literary inspirations, and the voyage apparently provided him with one or perhaps two dramas and a long prose romance. More tangible rewards did not materialize, for Lodge was soon in financial difficulty again.

The first drama, *The Wounds of Civil War,* is like Sackville and Norton's *Gorboduc* in its use of blank verse, long choral speeches, dumb shows, and Senecan violence. Paradise makes an admirable attempt to date the play, not printed until 1594, as 1586, before either of the more famous dramas it was thought to imitate: Marlowe's *Tamburlaine* (1587) and Kyd's *Spanish Tragedy* (c. 1586).[33] Although *The Wounds of Civil War* was probably acted in 1585 by the Admiral's Men, there are no records of its performance. But no matter what the date, the style shows none of Marlowe's brilliance in the line, and none of Kyd's machinations in the plot: but it does bear marks of *Gorboduc*—and of drama in general before the Golden Age was actually under way on the London stage. Our estimation of Lodge's first play must rely, therefore, on its date: if it preceded Marlowe, and the weight of circumstance seems to indicate that it did, the drama becomes more acceptable as a step between *Gorboduc* and *Tamburlaine*. If it followed *Tamburlaine,* it becomes no more than a poor imitation.

Two elements stand out in the play: its badly woven plot, and its surprising passages of lyric excellence. Little time need be spent on Lodge's plot; it simply is not well done, which may not be entirely Lodge's fault: he, like so many other play-wrights, followed his historical source. In this case, it was not the venerable Plutarch, as many thought; Lodge followed the *Roman Wars* of Appian, historian of the second century, who had been translated by "W.B." in 1578.[34] Apparently this translation was in large part Lodge's source.[35]

In any case, the see-saw movements of Marius and Scilla for power in Rome are mechanical and lack inspiration. Marius' achievements in Rome and Scilla's victories in Asia are duly reported; the struggle between them is finally resolved when Scilla conquers Rome and Marius commits suicide. There are too many episodes, too many characters, and too little motivation for what they do. The play lacks the excitement and suspense which Elizabethans came to demand of their drama.

The poetry of the drama shows some power, and an example is the Tribune's opening speech describing Marius in lines with Shakespearian tones:

> See Marius that in managing estate,
> Through many cares and troubles he hath past,
> And spent his youth, upon whose reuerend head
> The milke-white pledge of wisedome sweetly spreds:
> He sixe times Consul, fit for peace or warre,
> Sits drooping here content to brooke disgrace,
> Who glad to fight through follies of his foes
> Sighs for your shame whilst you abide secure.[36]

Readers must agree that many of Lodge's lines are tiresomely end stopped, but they must also concur that this passage is good blank verse. And Lodge is equally capable of the well-turned metaphor:

> For although Marius be renownd in Armes,
> Famous for prowesse, and graue in warlike drifts,
> Yet may the sunne-shine of his former deeds
> Nothing eclipse our Scilla's dignity.
>
> (I, i, 55–58, p. 4)

Scilla, who invariably gets the good lines, is like a Tamburlaine, though still a Roman:

This Capitoll wherein your glories shine,
Was nere so prest and throngde with scarlet gownes,
As Rome shall be with heapes of slaughtred soules,
Before that Scilla yeeld his titles vp.
Ile mate her streets that peere into the clouds,
Burnisht with gold and Iuorie pillors faire,
Shining with Iasper, Iet, and Ebonie,
All like the pallace of the morning sunne,
To swim within a sea of purple blood
Before I loose the name of Generall.
                              (I, i, 223–32, p. 9)

Marius only once rivals Scilla in his speeches. At his most mag-
nanimous moment, he frees Fulvia and Cornelia, Scilla's wife
and daughter, in lines full of romantic place names which poets
from Chaucer on have loved to write:

The bands that sould combine your snow white wrests,
Are these which shall adorne your milke white necks:
The priuate cells where you shall end your liues,
Is Italy, is Europe, nay the world:
Th' Euxinian sea, and fierce Sicilian Gulph,
The riuer Ganges and Hydaspis streame,
Shall level lye, and smoothe as christall yce:
Whilst Fuluia and Cornelia passe thereon:
The souldiers that should guard you to your deaths,
Shall be fiue thousand gallant youths of Rome,
In purple roabes crosse bard with pales of gold,
Mounted on warlike coursers for the field,
Fet from the mountaine tops of Cortia,
Or bred in hills of bright Sardinia,
Who shall conduct and bring you to your Lord,
I, vnto Scilla Ladies shall you goe. . . .
                              (IV, i, 1711–27, p. 52)

Lodge was a poet; as a dramatist, he had yet to prove himself.

V A Looking Glass for London and England

In the difficult years of the 1580's Lodge apparently had one
friend in Robert Greene. The extent of their friendship is not
known, but they were close enough to collaborate on A Look-

ing Glass for London and England; and later, while Lodge was on his way to the New World, Greene saw some of his friend's works through the press. There is no agreement on the date of this play, but it was probably written within a year of Lodge's *Wounds of Civil War,* probably 1587.[37] We do know that *A Looking Glass* was a popular attraction: Philip Henslowe reports that it was played four times at the Rose Theater early in 1592,[38] and it was printed in no less than five quarto editions by 1617.[39]

The drama is heavily moral, with strong biblical tones. It therefore appealed to the Londoners, for it capitalized on the mystery-miracle play theme and pointedly told the destruction of Nineveh, a faintly veiled London. The framework of the play is the evil of Rasni, King of Nineveh, and his counselor, Radagon, both of whom revel in incest, murder, and other crimes. Subplots show the machinations of usurers, corrupt judges, and drunken workingmen who allow their families to starve. After each scene of some new outrage by Rasni, Radagon, or the citizens of Nineveh, the prophet Hosea condemns not the preceding scene, but the parallel situation in London. The allegory is, therefore, only too plain. As Hosea's task is completed, Jonah arrives fresh from adventures inside the whale to deliver the last warning to Rasni: forty days before destruction. In a dramatically unmotivated scene, Rasni and his cohorts repent; the infamous usurer almost commits suicide for his sins; and Rasni appears in sackcloth. The turn is so sudden that even the divine workings of the deity could hardly seem an adequate explanation.

The final scenes of the drama include Jonah's curse on the withered vine and the appearance of the angel to spare the city. Jonah delivers his farewell, urging Rasni and the others to go forward and to do good works. The usurer gives back property to the rightful owners, and all is well. As is his custom in the play, Jonah turns to London to deliver a final warning reinforcing the theme that Hosea had chanted during the whole play:

O London, mayden of the mistresse Ile,
Wrapt in the foldes and swathing cloutes of shame . . .

[*43*]

London awake, for feare the Lord do frowne,
I set a looking Glasse before thine eyes.
O turne, O turne, with weeping to the Lord,
And thinke the praiers and vertues of thy Queene,
Defers the plague which otherwise would fall.
Repent O London, least for thine offence,
Thy shepheard faile, whom mightie God preserue,
That she may bide the pillar of his Church,
Against the stormes of Romish Anti-Christ:
The hand of mercy ouershead her head,
And let all faithfull subjects say, Amen.
                              (ll. 2388–89, 2399–2409)[40]

The drama included the satire, comedy, and stage excitement
which delighted the Elizabethans. The Jonah scenes in particular would have excited the audience, and these qualities, along
with the already mentioned strong moral message directed to
the court, accounted for the drama's popularity. The hand of
Greene is plainly seen: the play is much unlike Lodge's
Wounds of Civil War, and much like Greene's plays, such as
Friar Bacon and Friar Bungay. Greene wrote the final speech;
it is unlikely that Lodge, whose sympathies were now Roman,
would have written a line like "Against the stormes of Romish
Anti-Christ." But it is very likely that Lodge wrote the usurer
scenes since he had had firsthand acquaintance with these people as their victim.

Explorations in drama produced, however, no connection
with the world for Lodge. He was still searching, still striving
toward a goal as a literary man. His name was known, he had
proven himself as a pleasing imitator of Lyly's euphuistic style
in prose, and he had established himself in a small way as a
writer of some excellent poetry; but his talents were largely
unrecognized. The next few years were, however, to determine
his success as a writer.

CHAPTER 3

Triumphs and Troubles

AFTER lukewarm adventures with the London theaters, Thomas Lodge turned to the other forms of writing—prose and verse narratives, and lyrics—with which his contemporaries were meeting some success. During the years 1589–92, Lodge turned out some of his best lyrics and published two narratives: *Scillaes Metamorphosis* and *Rosalynde*. Of Lodge's longer works, these are certainly the best known. The *Metamorphosis* abounds in what one expects of Elizabethan verse, and the *Rosalynde* remains nonpareil among Elizabethan prose narratives. These two productions ought to have assured his future as a writer — they did not.

I Scillaes Metamorphosis

Scillaes Metamorphosis, or *Glaucus and Scilla* (1589) as it is sometimes called, allows us to see Lodge for the first time as a full-fledged poet.[1] The volume is entirely poetry, containing the much-sought Elizabethan variety—long verse narrative and lyrics in various forms. How long Lodge worked on the volume is not known since the appended poems reflect early experiments, but the *Metamorphosis* is late, certainly after the fruitless attempts at drama.

The story is of Glaucus, a sea god, who comes to the banks of the Thames while mourning his unhappy affair with the ever-changing nymph, Scilla. He pours out his tale to the poet, then both go to Sicily to see Love's revenge on the vacillating Scilla, who is condemned to remain on the rock which bears her name, according to the tradition in Ovid's *Metamorphoses*. The subject, is, therefore, Ovidian and erotic; and the transition from *Truth's Complaint* to this narrative illustrates the whole trend of Elizabethan poetry. The *Complaint* is diverse, heavily didactic, appallingly outdated; the *Metamorphosis* is rich, concentrated, and only by the greatest stretch of imagination is it moral. The "detestable tyrannie of Disdaine, and Comicall triumph of Constancie" are certainly present, but they are overshadowed by the torrents of description and images which pour out, even obscuring the sober Medieval figures of Furie, Rage, Wan-Hope, Dispaire, and Woe which appear momentarily at the end of the poem.

The shift in emphasis from Medieval to Renaissance style had been evolving for some time; and it depends on Ovid and the interpretation of his works. Early in the Christian era Ovid, as much as Virgil, was subjected to allegorical analysis; and the remnants of Ovid which drifted into England from various Continental sources retained allegorical flavor. Ovid, who was deemed somewhat immoral, could not be interpreted literally; but, if taken allegorically, the most pious and conscience-stricken of Christians could read Salmacis and Hermaphroditus and not only remain pure in heart but could be edified. In fact, Dante illustrates the trend by placing Ovid in limbo with Homer, Horace, and Lucan.

Douglas Bush has outlined the Continental background of this type of Ovidian allegory which came to England.[2] Arthur Golding, the English authority because of his translation of the *Metamorphoses* (1567), gave Ovid most exalted praise in the preface, probably because he was sincere, or perhaps, as has been suggested, for fear of censors.[3] Golding and others gave widespread license to raid Ovid, but the resulting literature was to have a moral appended; for, if anyone believes the Elizabethans were not moral, no matter by what route they reached their morality, he has misread his authors. Lodge, the first writer to solidify these tendencies and attitudes, made use of Golding's ideas and, of even more importance, of a translation of the story of Salmacis-Hermaphroditus by Thomas Peend, published in 1565, a translation which inspired another anonymous version in 1602. As Hallett Smith notes, Peend expands the incident and elaborates on it with an attack on women.[4] The 1602 translation presents a "general effect . . . of irresponsible delight, with variety, color, and lightness of touch."[5]

The young men at Lincoln's Inn knew Golding and Peend,

although Lodge would not have seen the anonymous 1602 edition; they knew Ovid; what was needed was the mind and the ability to draw out of these raw materials a new form which was not merely a translation with appended morals. Lodge did just this: in his preface he preserved the moral purpose in the recommendation, "verie fit for young Courtiers to peruse, and coy dames to remember," and in the epigraph "*O vita! misero longa, foelici breuis*"; and in the poem he combined this morality with at least some of the spirit of Ovid to create a poem which is rich in color and variety, and yet instructs young Courtiers and coy dames without becoming a sermon.

Lodge had not intended to release *Scillaes Metamorphosis* at the time it appeared. The work, which was circulated in manuscript, fell into the hands of a printer, Richard Jones, who published it. Such piracy was common among Elizabethan printers, and writers had to defend themselves without the aid of laws to protect their interests. Lodge's defense is in the dedication of the work to Ralph Crane, a fellow at Lincoln's Inn; but since these these dedications contain some of the best subjective biographical information available, we also learn that Lodge's "discontented thoughts" have been "long inured to obscuritie." Lodge is bitter:

Our wits now a daies are waxt verie fruitefull, and our Pamphleters more than prodigall; So that the postes which stoode naked a tedious *non terminus*, doo vaunt their double apparrel as soone as euer the Exchequer openeth; and euerie corner is tooke vp with some or other penilesse companion that will imitate any estate for a twopennie almes. I could afford you whole seruices of absurdities, that would disquiet the digestion of Arte *vsq; ad nausæam*, were it not that I pittie to particularize simple fellowes imperfections, and am altogether loath to aduenture my paines in so vngratefull a Prouince.[6]

Writing is "vaine glories inordinate follie" and Glaucus exerts the following promise from the poet:

> At last he left me, where at first he found me,
> Willing me let the world and ladies knowe
> Of Scillas pride, and then by oath he bound me

To write no more, of that whence shame dooth grow:
Or tie my pen to *Pennie-knaues* delight,
But liue with fame, and so far fame to wright.
(ll. 773–78, p. 28)

Lodge also tells us in his dedication that the title of the poem proper is "The most pithie and pleasant *Historie of Glaucus and Scilla.*" In its purest essence, "pithie and pleasant" describes almost all of Elizabethan poetry. Ovid, at the conclusion of Book XIII, the wanderings of the Trojans, tells the history of Scilla and Charybdis; Scilla's meeting with Glaucus begins at line 898 and runs to the seventy-fourth line of Book XIV, a total of one hundred forty-four lines. Lodge's poem, including Glaucus' complaint, is eight hundred thirty-eight lines. The spirit of embellishment which gave us Chaucer's *Troilus and Criseyde* in the fourteenth century was, therefore, not dead in the sixteenth. Lodge's verse form—the traditional quatrain capped with a couplet—borrows much from rime royal and ottava rima, and lends much to Shakespeare's sonnet form. The stanza appears occasionally before Lodge, but never in narrative poetry. Thomas, Lord Vaux, had written a lyric in this stanza for Richard Edward's *Paradise of Dainty Devices* (1576).[7] Gascoigne, George Whetstone, the Earl of Oxford, Sir Edward Dyer, and others had composed some of the loveliest lyrics in this form before Lodge; but no writer put it to such sustained use. Although the stanza has since become famous through Shakespeare's *Venus and Adonis,* the effect of the stanza in *Glaucus and Scilla,* sustained through almost eight hundred lines, is like a series of miniature sonnets. For the quatrain-couplet lends much more the effect of exposition-resolution than either rime royal or ottava rima. The drawback is that the stanza is not well suited to tense narrative, but neither Lodge nor Shakespeare was deeply interested in narrative; they wanted to embellish an old tale; the art of invention had not yet struck them.

As is always true in Lodge, parts are better than the whole. Many single stanzas and some passages are among the finest poetry Elizabethan England produced; other parts are drab—a problem of many poems: Spenser, Shakespeare, Milton, and

Wordsworth write many a dull passage between the bright spots. However, Lodge is guilty of a weak beginning, for which Horace would have taxed him: "semper ad eventum festinat et in medias res / non secus ac notas auditorem rapit, et quae / desperat tractata nitescere posse, relinquit. . . ." [8] But the loveliness of the pastoral, quasi-medieval dream setting soon makes us forget *in medias res*:

> And as I sat vnder a Willow tree,
> The louelie honour of faire *Thetis* bower;
> Reposd his head vpon my faintfull knee:
> And when my teares had ceast their stormie shower
> He dried my cheekes, and then bespake him so,
> As when he waild I straight forgot my woe.
> (ll. 13–18, p. 7)

Lodge is taking his readers nowhere in a hurry; this is a leisurely complaint, disguised ever so well by riches from the Continental poets. Until the really descriptive passages following line 50, we are much in the old complaint world, which celebrated the miseries of this "vale of tears." "Marke how the morne in roseat colour shines, / And straight with cloudes the Sunnie tract is clad; / Then see how pomp through waxe and waine declines. . . ." (ll. 25–27, p. 7) Or: "Conclude and knowe times change by course of fate, / Then mourne no more, but moane my haples state." (ll. 41–42, p. 8)

After line 50 the gods and nymphs troop in, and we are in another sphere:

> Vpon the siluer bosome of the streame
> First gan faire *Themis* shake her amber locks,
> Whom all the Nimphs that waight on *Neptunes* realme
> Attended from the hollowe of the rocks.
>   In briefe, while these rare parragons assemble,
>   The watrie world to touch their teates doo tremble.
> (ll. 55–60, p. 8)

These examples might be called a marriage of the best of two styles—Medieval complaint and Renaissance lavishness—but I think it is merely a confusion of them. Lodge was aware of current trends among the young writers at the Inns of Court, and he attempted to capture all possible readers. The familiar complaint frame would attract the traditionalists; the sensuous displays in description would appeal to the younger readers eager for new styles.

After the nymphs and gods depart, the scene is clearly pastoral:

> Ay me, the Shepheards let their flockes want feeding
> And flockes to see their palie face are sorie,
> The Nimphes to spie the flocks and shepheards needing
> Prepare their teares to heare our tragicke storie:
>   Whilst we surprisde with griefe cannot disclose them
>   With sighing wish the world for to suppose them.
> (ll. 115–20, p. 10)

Lodge encompassed every possible taste for Medieval adherrents and Renaissance stylists early in the poem, and he culminates the introduction with this splendid passage which Shakespeare imitated in *Venus and Adonis:*

> He that hath seene the sweete *Arcadian* boy
> Wiping the purple from his forced wound,
> His pretie teares betokening his annoy,
> His sighes, his cries, his falling on the ground,
>   The Ecchoes ringing from the rockes his fall,
>   The trees with teares reporting of his thrall:
>
> And *Venus* starting at her loue-mates crie,
> Forcing her birds to hast her chariot on;
> And full of griefe at last with piteous eie
> Seene where all pale with death he lay alone,
>   Whose beautie quaild, as wont the Lillies droop
>   When wastful winter windes doo make them stoop:
>
> Her daintie hand addrest to dawe her deere,
> Her roseall lip alied to his pale cheeke,
> Her sighes, and then her lookes and heauie cheere,
> Her bitter threates, and then her passions meeke;
>   How on his senseles corpes she lay a crying,
>   As if the boy were then but new a dying.
> (ll. 121–38, p. 10)

Then follows a summary of Ariosto's *Orlando Furioso* (1516, 1532) in three stanzas, and references to other women who lost their lovers, leading to Scilla, who scorns Glaucus. Not until Themis has brought Moly, a fabulous curative herb, and Glaucus has prefaced his story with another long complaint does the narrative really begin: it has taken Lodge two hundred and seventy-five lines to reach the point where Ovid begins.

The Classical tradition of cataloguing, inherited from Homer and Virgil, became a vehicle for describing women's charms; shortly after the narrative proper is underway, Lodge describes Scilla: "Her haire not trust, but scatterd on her brow, / Surpassing *Hiblas* honnie for the view, / Or softned golden wires . . . ; (ll. 283–85; p. 15) and, "An yuorie shadowed front, wherein was wrapped / Those pretie bowres where Graces couched be: / Next which her cheekes appeerd like crimson silk, / Or ruddie rose bespred on whitest milk." (ll. 291–94, p. 15).

When the action comes, it is over quickly; and Glaucus again complains of Scilla's unfaithfulness as Lodge brings the time to the present situation. Thetis, Glaucus' mother, appears to console her son. A prayer is offered to Venus, marked by the recurring line, "assist poore *Glaucus* late by Loue undone," and Venus appears to answer. The stage is set for another description, and the picture Lodge gives us is disturbingly like Renaissance paintings of the madonna:

> Delicious louely shine her prettie eies,
> And one her cheekes carnatioon cloudes arise . . .
> And on her lap her louely Sonne was plaste,
> Whose beautie all his mothers pomp defaste.
> A wreath of roses hem'd his Temples in,
> His tresse was curlde and cleere as beaten gold.
> (ll. 507–8; 513–16, p. 21)

Cupid's cure is immediately effective, as in Ovid; and Scilla's appearance on the scene allows another description. Wounded now, she pursues Glaucus: "Lord how her lippes doo dwell vpon his cheekes / And how she lookes for babies in his eies: / And how she sighes, and sweares shee loues and

leekes, / And how she vowes, and he her vowes enuies. . . ."
(ll. 617–20, p. 24).

As she cannot succeed in winning his love, she complains;
and, complaining, she is pursued to her rock, where an Ovidian
Echo scene follows. The end of the poem reverts to a list of
Medieval allegorical figures: Furie, Rage, Wan-Hope, Dispaire,
and Woe are described as they might be in a catalogue of the
seven deadly sins:

> *Woe* all in blacke, within his hands did beare
> The fatall torches of a Funerall,
> Her Cheeks were wet, dispearsed was hir heare,
> Her voice was shrill (yet loathsome therewith all):
> *Wan-Hope* (poore soule) on broken Ancker sitts,
> Wringing his armes as robbed of his witts.
>
> (ll. 725–30, p. 27)

Such a sketch hardly convinces the skeptical of any great
development beyond Sackville's contribution to the *Mirror for
Magistrates;* but the sustained Ovidian passages, the lush descriptions, the sonnet conventions in imagery soon convince the
reader that Lodge has gone beyond Sackville's "Induction."
"The innovation in Lodge's poem is that it does not treat the
myth as an allegory." [9] Ovid is Ovid; description is sensuous; it
does not represent anything else. The "erotic and pictorial aspects" are developed as ends in themselves. [10] Lodge gave several older genres—the pastoral, the love complaint, the Medieval narrative, the Ovidian allegory—what they lacked: ". . .
what the mythological poem needed if it was to rise above the
feeble paraphrases and moralizations of Ovid was the influence
of continental art and style." [11] This Lodge accomplished, but
he also "shows himself to have been a poet of real power who
had not quite attained full stature." [12] Lodge's full stature would
come; at this stage, the best summary is that "in poetic feeling,
Glaucus and Scilla has a new quality which forecasts the faerie
world of Spenser." [13]

II   Discontented Satyre *and "Sundrie Sweete Sonnets"*

The *Glaucus Complaint* appended to the *Metamorphosis* is
an insignificant addition which Lodge could not find space for

in the narrative proper, but it might well have been an early
version out of which the longer poem grew. Of considerably
more interest is the *Discontented Satyre* which follows the
Complaint. John Peter finds this poem a prelude to Lodge's
later Roman satires: ". . . we have something of an augury for
later poems by the author: one who professed to admire Discontent was not likely to avoid the satirist's role for long." [14]

Written in the same six-line stanzas, the poem in some one
hundred lines sustains the gloomiest of malcontent tones. The
opening stanzas describe night and relate it to the poet's feelings: "The doaly season that resembled well / My drooping
heart, gaue life to my lament." [15] The poet wanders into a "de-
sert dale" where the satyr complains: "Boast Discontent,
naught may depresse thy powre, / Since in thy selfe all griefe
thou doost deuoure. / Thou art the God whome I alone
adore / Whose powre includeth discords all in one. . . ." (ll.
41–44, p. 32) Princes, soldiers, artists, all reach truth through
discontent; even the philosopher is included: "The schooleman
that with heedlesse florish writes, / Refines his fault, if thou direct his eie: / And then again with wonder he endites / Such
sweete sententious lines, as neuer die." (ll. 91–94, p. 33) After
such lessons, the poet "with watch forespent / Drew home and
vowde to honor Discontent."

The volume concludes with "Sundrie Sweete Sonnets," some
sixteen poems with running titles "Delectable Poems" and "Delectable Sonnets" which had accumulated in the poet's note-
books since his Oxford days. Lyrics, experimental in meter and
in form borrowed from the Continental poets, show the influence of outside trends among the Elizabethans, and the gropings for new styles. The four longer poems of the group range
from the conventional "praise of the Country life"—modeled
on Horace's *Satires* II, vi; Wyatt's "Of the Mean and Sure Estate"; and more directly, as L. E. Kastner has noted, on the
opening chanson of Philippe Desportes' *Bergeries*,[16]—to "In
commendation of the solitarie life," which has some biographical hints of the stand Lodge was to take within a few years on
his literary career: "Since where content and wealthie state declines, / The heart doth droope, and dolefull be the lines";[17]
and

What fruites of former labours doo I finde?
My studious pen dooth traffique for a scorne:
My due deserts are but repaid with winde:
And what I earne, is nought but bitter mourne:
  In which accompt I reap but this aduise,
  To cease to clime and liue contented wise.

(ll. 13–18, p. 37)

Lodge was moving toward the urbane, satiric vein which
would culminate in poetry with *A Fig for Momus* and in prose
with *A Margarite of America*.

Beauties Lullabie contains a headnote which attests to further activities of pirates: *"Hos ego versiculos feci, tulit alter
honores.* Gentlemen, I had thought to haue suppressed this
Lullabie in silence, amongst my other papers that lie buried in
obliuion: but the impudent arrogancie of some more then inso-
lent Poets haue altered my purpose in that respect, and made
me set my name to my owne worke, least some other vain
glorious *Batillus* should preiudice my paines, by subscribing his
name to that which is none of his owne." [18]

The *Lullabie* is a long, very conventional description of the
poet's mistress in lines varying in meter from six to eight
stresses. Lodge called the experiment *non mesureè*. One line
suffices to illustrate the path of progress from hair to toes—
"Next lulla to those lamps, those twinckling stemmes of state"—
which reminds the reader of Spenser's *Amoretti* LXXVII and
many others.

The twelve "sonnets" which follow are certainly experimental, and they remind the reader of Thomas Watson's *Hecatom-
pathia* in variety of form and meter. As Paradise noted, "The
'Sundrie sweete sonnets' are little more than experiments in
technique and were clearly written before the sonnet form had
been established in England." [19] The poems range in length
from ten to thirty-two lines, from tetrameters to hexameters,
and from lovers' complaints to lovers' joys in conventional
manner. Paradise noted resemblances between some of Lodge's
work and that of his contemporaries; but because dates of
composition are uncertain, no specific theory of influence or of
imitation is possible.[20] One of these experiments closely resem-
bles a similar attempt by Robert Greene, "Francescoes Rounde-

lay." Lodge's "When with advice I weigh my yeares forepast" [21] ends each stanza with a refrain—"I loath the faults and follies of mine eie"—that is much like Greene's "Wo worth the faults and follies of mine eie."

A more striking resemblance lies between Lodge's "I will become a Hermit now" and Sir Walter Raleigh's "Like to a Hermite poore in place obscure." Raleigh's poem reads:

> Like to a Hermite poore in place obscure,
> I meane to spend my daies of endles doubt,
> To waile such woes as time cannot recure,
> Where none but Loue shall euer finde me out.
>
> My foode shall be of care and sorow made.
> My drink nought else but teares falne from mine eies,
> And for my light in such obscured shade,
> The flames shall serue, which from my hart arise.
>
> A gowne of graie, my bodie shall attire,
> My staffe of broken hope whereon Ile staie,
> Of late repentance linckt with long desire,
> The couch is fram'de whereon my limbs Ile lay,
>
> And at my gate dispaire shall linger still,
> To let in death when Loue and Fortune will.[22]

Lodge's fourth poem is similar:

> I will become a Hermit now,
>   and doo my penance straight
> For all the errors of mine eyes
>   with foolish rashnes fild:
> My hermitage shall placed be,
>   where melancholies waight,
> And none but loue alone shall knowe
>   the bower I meane to build.
> My daylie diet shall be care,
>   made calme by no delight:
> My dolefull drinke my drierie teares,
>   amidst the darksome place
> The fire that burnes my heedles heart
>   shall stand in stead of light,

And shall consume my wearie life
    mine errors to deface.
My gowne shall be of spreading gray
    to clad my limmes withall:
My late repent vpon my browe
    shall plainlie written be.
My tedious griefe and great remorse
    that doth my soule enthrall,
Shall serue to plead my wearie paines
    and pensiue miserie.
Of fainfull hope shall be my staffe,
    and daylie when I pray,
My mistris picture plac't by loue
    shall witnes what I say.[23]

Lyrics such as these circulated in manuscript among young writers; and, as a good many were never intended for publication, it is not surprising that one man imitated another's subject.

A good deal of scholarship has been expended on the sources for these "sonnets" for the *Phillis* sequence, and for much of what Lodge and his contemporaries wrote. The resemblances above make one thing clear: Lodge and his fellow writers imitated in the true sense of that word. As we noted in Chapter 1, they imitated each other, and they imitated their Continental counterparts. The direction of research into sources is, therefore, in question: if it is directed with the purpose of illustrating the flow of Renaissance thought from Italy to England, it is good; when the aim seems to be merely to point out the victim's lack of imagination for inventing subject matter, themes, and forms, then the scholarship becomes useless. We seem to rely too much on the Romantic credo that the imagination is the true source for the poet's inspiration and to forget Aristotle and Horace on imitation. Scaliger and Bruno in Italy, and Sidney in England followed the doctrine of imitation. It is unwise, therefore, to apply twentieth-century standards to earlier literature.

It has been pointed out in a succession of articles how much Lodge, without giving any credit, relied on the Italians, or on Ronsard and Desportes. Why this borrowing should suddenly become a major crime in 1590 after what Chaucer and John Gower borrowed is puzzling. We have seen how standards shift: if succeeding ages grant the laurel, such words as "plagiarize," "plunder," and "servile imitation" disappear from critics' notes; if the ages grant only dust, the critics are free to crucify.

A much saner approach is to look at the English poem, evaluate our impressions, and then, as an interesting analogue, look at its predecessors. If the English poem is "good," we should not care if the poet borrowed it from a Continental contemporary—just as we do not judge the art of Shakespeare's plays on the sources. An example is Lodge's "In Praise of the Solitary Life" noted above. As an expression of the feelings of the poet, whether French or English, it is good. Desportes' chanson is "good"—in French. And if the French source hunters are as agile as the English, they have found Desportes in debt to an Italian poet, the Italian to a Greek, *ad infinitum.*

Of the twelve sonnets in the *Scilla* group, it has faithfully been shown that four have close parallels with Desportes' *Bergeries.*[24] On the basis of such evidence, we might conclude, if we were so disposed, that the rest have parents elsewhere. On the other hand, a reader might simply enjoy the eleventh, borrowed or not:

> A Satyre sitting by a riuer side,
> Foreworne with care that hardlie findes recure:
> A straying Nymph in passion did deride
> His teares, his care, her smiles her scornes assure:
>> He wept, she wisht, and all their thoughts among,
>> Fancie beheld and sung this carefull song.
> Perhaps the furrowes in thy wrinckled face
> Growne by thy griefe, abate thy wonted forme:
> Perhaps her eye was formde to yeeld disgrace,
> And blemisht that which wit may not reforme.
>> Perhaps she will if so thou list to proue,
>> Perhaps she likes, and yet she dares not loue.
> But if (perhaps) thy fortune be so faire,
> Laugh Satyre then it proues a pretie prize:
> And if thou wilt, so liue to shun dispaire
> As looking long thou keepe thy proper eyes.

> This said she ceast: the Nymph she fled away,
> And good perswasion causde the Satyre play.[25]

The *Metamorphosis* volume marks, in many ways, both the beginning and the end of Lodge's literary career. There is certainly evidence that he was disappointed at the poor success thus far of his efforts, and there is evidence that Lodge had real poetic powers, ones just emerging from the doleful tenor of fifteenth century modes, and just touching the golden lights of the Continental Renaissance.

III Rosalynde

Certainly one of the golden lights of the English Renaissance is *Rosalynde,* the one work for which Lodge will always be remembered, if, at times, in a rather secondhand way. The genesis of the work is reported by Lodge: "Hauing with Capt. Clarke made a voyage to the Islands of Terceras and the Canaries, to beguile the time with labour I writ this book; rough, as hatcht in the stormes of the ocean, and feathered in the surges of many perilous seas." [26]

The work is dedicated to Henry Carey, Lord Hunsdon, one of the most prominent warrior-courtiers of Elizabeth's court; Lodge was groping for patronage, and the whole tone of the epistle is that of a soldier. Lodge, flushed with the relative success of his play written with Greene and with the reception of *Scilla's Metamorphosis,* had just returned from his successful voyage to the Canaries; and the dedication spills over with the confidence and self-assurance which would lead him to address a great soldier in this fashion: "When I entered, right honorable, with deep insight into the consideration of these premises, seeing your L. to be a Patron of all martial men, and a Moecenas of such as apply themselues to study; wearing with Pallas both the launce and the bay, and ayming with Augustus at the fauour of all, by the honorable vertues of your mind: being my selfe first a Student, and after falling from bookes to armes, euen vowed in all my thoughts dutifully to affect your L." [27] Through his acquaintance with Lord Hunsdon's sons Edmund and Robert Carey, Lodge presumed to attract the attention of the great nobleman.

The epistle to "the Gentlemen Readers" contains more assurance of his powers as a writer; he warns them:

If you like it, so: and yet I will be yours in duetie, if you be mine in fauour. But if Momus or any squint-eyed asse, that hath mighty ears to conceiue with Midas, and yet little reason to iudge; if he come aboord our Barke to find fault with the tackling, when he knows not the shrowdes, Ile down into the hold, and fetch out a rustie Pollax, that saw no sunne this seauen year, and either well bast him, or heaue the cockscombe ouer boord to feed cods.[28]

This tone is somewhat different from that of previous dedications and epistles. The "take it or leave it" attitude is growing in Lodge. The half successes and half failures of his publications were beginning to gall, and he attempted in his new sailor's jargon to make a firm stand and a firm appeal as a writer. The next few years would furnish the results; for the present, his *Rosalynde* achieved its purpose.

The history of romance and its popularity in Elizabethan England have been mentioned in the discussion of *Forbonius and Prisceria* in Chapter 2. Many attempts had been made to define a form and a style for romance, but, as we have seen, Lyly's *Euphues* for style and Sidney's *Arcadia* for form made up the formula for this popular genre. Lodge's work, however, becomes an aristocrat, so excellent it exceeds both progenitors. Lyly's style is tempered: "a style which is closely related to those of *Euphues* and the *Arcadia*, but which has more color and warmth and more flexibility than Lyly's." [29] And the plot form of Sidney's *Arcadia* is encompassed so that the reader can grasp the situations easily. The excursions into side lines which so exasperate the reader of the *Arcadia* or of Greene's romances are absent; the reader is at home with Lodge, who sticks to his purpose, style, and moral in a simple tale: "'Rosalind' . . . is the flower of Elizabethan romance. It satisfies some of the usual terms in the modern definition of the novel. For it is of reasonable length; it possesses a kind of structure, and closes with an elaborate moral." [30] Lodge, therefore, capitalized on the success of his contemporaries and produced the *Rosalynde* which has endured as a favorite romance; eight editions appeared in Lodge's lifetime, and others have continued to appear.

The plot in general is that of the *Tale of Gamelyn,* a fourteenth-century romance long attributed to Chaucer. Rosader, an ill-treated younger brother, and Rosalynde, daughter of a wrongfully exiled duke, meet at a wrestling match in which Rosader is victorious. Their difficulties force them to flee separately to the forest of Arden, Rosalynde disguised as a page. Their adventures in love and in reconciliation among the rustics in the pastoral setting provide all the ingredients of a warmly human romance.

Lodge's lyrics—some twenty-two poems "of the finest order of excellence" [31]—add much to the success of *Rosalynde.* Sonnets in varying lengths, eclogues, and madrigals pour from the characters in a splendid array. "Several of Lodge's best songs are included . . ." [32] and their popularity is attested by their presence in *England's Helicon* (1600) and thereafter in Renaissance anthologies.[33] There is much simple beauty in a song like "Rosalynds Madrigal": the language is uncomplicated, and the images are homely. The paradoxes of love—delight and sorrow—are traditional, but the plaintive note in a line like "Ah wanton, will ye?" and the surrender in "Spare not but play thee" express the pleasure and pain of love clearly:

> Loue in my bosome like a Bee
> doth sucke his sweete:
> Now with his wings he playes with me
> now with his feet.
> Within mine eies he makes his neast,
> His bed amidst my tender breast,
> My kisses are his daily feast;
> And yet he robs me of my rest,
> Ah wanton, will ye?
>
> And if I sleepe, then pearcheth he
> with pretie flight,
> And makes his pillow of my knee
> the liuelong night.
> Strike I my lute he tunes the string,
> He musicke playes if so I sing,
> He lends me euerie louelie thing;

> Yet cruell he my heart doth sting.
>   Whist wanton still ye?
>
> Els I with roses euerie day
>   will whip you hence;
> And binde you when you long to play,
>   for your offence.
>   Ile shut mine eyes to keepe you in,
>   Ile make you fast it for your sinne,
>   Ile count your power not worth a pinne;
>   Ahlas what hereby shall I winne,
>   If he gainsay me?
>
> What if I beate the wanton boy
>   with manie a rod?
> He will repay me with annoy,
>   because a God.
>   Then sit thou safely on my knee,
>   And let thy bowre my bosome be:
>   Lurke in mine eyes I like of thee:
> Oh *Cupid* so thou pitie me,
>   Spare not but play thee.[34]

In almost any lyric Lodge is particularly good; in the following stanza the meter gives an urgency to the lover's description:

> *Phoebe* sat
> By a fount;
>   Sitting by a fount I spide her:
> Sweet her touch
> Rare her voyce;
>   Touch and voice what may distaine you? [35]

In the refrain from "Phoebe's Sonnet" the lover's dejection is combined with a traditional refrain from old folk songs:

>   Downe a downe
> Thus Phillis sung
>   by fancie once distressed:
> Who so by foolish loue are stung,
>   Are worthely oppressed.
>   And so sing I. With a downe a downe, downe;[36]

The "sonnetto" added to one of Phoebe's letters illustrates again the plaintive note in love, but with restraint:

> Time hath subdued arte,
> and ioy is slaue to woe:
> Alas (Loue's guide) be kind;
> what shall I perish so? [37]

Lodge experimented with a variety of lyric forms ranging from short to long lines, from traditional to invented stanzas, and from conventional to unorthodox line arrangements. The more unusual forms are illustrated in these lines:

> Gentle Loue
> Lowre no more
> if thou wilt inuade.
> In the secret shade,
> Labour not so sore. . . . [38]

There are also a great many songs from the old ballad tradition, like this stanza with its refrain, repetition, and well-defined meter:

> A blyth and bonny country Lasse,
> heigh ho the bonny Lasse:
> Sate sighing on the tender grasse,
> and weeping said, will none come woo mee? [39]

The two eclogues of the *Rosalynde* are traditional: shepherds converse about the most sophisticated subjects while tending their sheep, just as they did in the *Idyls* of Theocritus. The most familiar subject is the poor relationship of lover and coy lass, as in Montanus and Coridon's eclogue in *Rosalynde*:

> Say shepheards boy, what makes thee greet so sore?
> Why leaues thy pipe his pleasure and delight?
> Yong are thy yeares, thy cheekes with roses dight:
> Then sing for ioy (sweet swaine) and sigh no more. [40]

Of some more interest is the "wooing Eglogue betwixt Rosalynde and Rosader" though the arguments between lover and reluctant lady are conventional:

> *Rosalynde.*
> The hardened steele by fire is brought in frame:
> *Rosader.*
> And *Rosalynde* my loue than anie wooll more softer;
> And shall not sighes her tender heart inflame?
> *Rosalynde.*
> Were louers true, maides would beleeue them ofter.
> *Rosader.*
> Truth and regard, and honour guide my loue.
> *Rosalynde.*
> Faine would I trust, but yet I dare not trie.
> *Rosader.*
> Oh pitie me sweete Nymph, and doo but proue.
> *Rosalynde.*
> I would resist, but yet I know not why.[41]

Although Lodge made further use of these experiments with eclogue form in *A Fig for Momus* (1595), and although he experimented with shorter lyrics throughout his writing career, the lyrics of *Rosalynde* are his finest effort. Paradise says of them: "He had by this time mastered the technique of verse writing, so that in several of these poetical interludes may be heard the true, effortless music of Elizabethan song at its best." [42] But not only the lyrics of *Rosalynde* draw our attention; the whole romantic tale is a delight. And this delight made Shakespeare create his masterpiece, for "Lodge must have the credit of the delightful story of *As You Like It*." [43] The debt is there, but Shakespeare's use of the story should not be the reason for enjoying *Rosalynde*.[44]

No one would deny the euphuistic style of *Rosalynde*, but all would agree Lodge has surpassed Lyly in common sense. The elements are on the first page—sentences carefully constructed for balance and parallelism: "There dwelled adioining to the city of Bourdeaux a Knight of most honorable parentage, whom Fortune had graced with many fauours, and Nature honored with sundry exquisite qualities, so beautified with the excellence of both, as it was a question whether Fortune or Nature were more prodigall in deciphering the riches of their bounties." [45] He uses the images from unnatural natural history: "Sir John, (that with the Phenix knewe the tearme of his life was now expyred, and could with the Swanne, discouer his end by her songs), hauing three sonnes, by his wife Lynida . . . thought now, (seeing death by constraint would compel him to leaue them), to bestow upon them such a Legacie as might bewray his loue, and increase thier ensuing amitie." [46]

So long as Lodge becomes no more involved, we are with him. Only occasionally does he drop his guard, and lapse back to Lyly's excesses of language, as in the will Sir John gives verbally to his sons: "Soare not with the Hobbie, least you fall with the Larke, nor attempt not with Phaeton, least you drowne with Icarus." [47] The reader must also concentrate as he reads the euphuistic "Saladyne's Meditation with himself," but, although these monologues are hard to read through, the apologist may argue that they form the basis of "character" novels. Saladyne, in the euphuistic tradition, rationalizes himself to the proper pitch, sustained with quotations from the classics: "What, tis not so olde as true: *Non sapit, qui sibi non sapit*. Thy Brother is young, keepe him now in awe, make him not check mate with thy selfe, for *Nimis familiaritas comtemptum parit*." [48] Although the monologues continue throughout the whole romance, Lodge saves this sluggish progress from scorn by adding his delightful lyrics. If Rosalynde spouts Latin maxims, she also sings "Loue in my bosome like a Bee."

As the company moves to the forest of Arden, Lodge releases his style from Lyly's clutches: the development of Rosalynde as an endearing lady of English literature leads Lodge away from excess, and the prose takes on a new sound. Rosalynde, as Ganymede, answers her companion well:

No doubt (quoth Aliena) this poesie is the passion of some perplexed shepheard, that being enamoured of some faire and beautifull Shepheardesse, suffered some sharpe repulse, and therefore complained of the crueltie of his Mistris. You may see (quoth Ganimede) what mad cattell you women be, whose hearts sometimes are made of Adamant that will touch with no impression, and sometime of waxe that is fit for euerie forme: they delight to be courted, and then they glorie to seem coy; and when they are most desired then they freese with disdaine: and this fault is so common to the sex, that you see it painted out in the shepheard's passions, who found his Mistris as froward as he was enamoured.

And I pray you (quoth Aliena) if your roabes were off, what mettall are you made of that you are so satyricale against women? Is it not a foule bird defiles the own nest? . . . Thus (quoth Ganimede) I keepe decorum, I speak now as I am Alienas page, not as I am Gerismonds daughter: for put me but into a peticoate, and I will stand in defiance to the vttermost, that women are courteous, constant, virtuous, and what not.[49]

Shakespeare's heroines have much of this mettle; the firm, defiant Renaissance lady emerges in literature with almost as much flair as the celebrated Renaissance man.

The best part of the romance is Rosalynde's disguise as Ganymede, playing herself for Rosader's benefit during the elaborate practice wooing that takes place, imaginary and real at the same time. At the conclusion of this artifice, Aliena, who knows all, says: "And thereupon (quoth Aliena) Ile play the priest, from this day forth Ganimede shall call thee husband, and thou shall call Ganimede wife, and weele haue a marriage. Content (quoth Rosader) and laught. Content (quoth Ganimede) and changed as redde as a rose: and so with a smile and a blush, they made vp this iesting match, that after prooued to a marriage in earnest; Rosader full little thinking he had wooed and wonne his Rosalynde." [50]

The pastoral scene dominates until all the problems are solved; the city, it seems, breeds difficulties with which only Arden can cope. When the battles are done, disguises discovered, and marriages completed, in one line Lodge makes all his main characters urban: "Well, as soon as they were come to Paris. . . ." The conclusion is moral, more than it need be, even for the Elizabethan reader. Lodge breaks the narrative and appears in person as he takes farewell in an epilogue:

Here, gentlemen, may you see in Euphues Golden Legacie, that such as neglect their fathers precepts, incurre much preiudice; that diuision in Nature as it is a blemish in nurture, so tis a breach of good fortunes; that vertue is not measured by birth but by action; that younger bretheren though inferior in yeares, yet may be superior to honours; that concord is the sweetest conclusion, and amitie betwixt brothers more forceable than fortune. If you gather any frutes by this Legacie, speake well of Euphues for writing it, and me for fetching it. If you grace me with that fauor, you encourage me to be more forward; and as soone as I haue ouerlookt my labours, expect the Sailer's Kalender.[51]

What the "Kalender" is we never find out, but we do find that Lodge brought English prose fiction of the romance genre to its highest development before the form died. The pastoral setting, the fanciful notions of lovers, the oppressions of cruel tyrants, and the lyric excellence of shepherds fall before the realistic prose of Thomas Nashe's *The Unfortunate Traveler* (1594) and Thomas Deloney's *Jack of Newbury* (1619). *Rosalynde* is the last and the best of prose romance.

CHAPTER 4

Searching

LODGE was excited by the reception of his *Rosalynde*—so excited that he worked hard during the next two years on two fronts: first, the success of *Rosalynde* brought about the writing of three prose works: *The Famous, true, and historicall life of Robert second Duke of Normandy*, and *Catharos, Diogenes in his Singularitie* were published in 1591; in 1592 *Euphues Shadow, the Battaile of the Senses* appeared. Secondly, Lodge embarked optimistically on a voyage to the New World with Sir Thomas Cavendish. He must have felt that his fortunes were on the upswing; but, characteristically, all the ventures, literary and military, ended without success.

I   Robert of Normandy

After the careful attention to style in *Rosalynde*, it is a distinct disappointment to turn to the slim volume containing both *Robert, Duke of Normandy* and *Catharos*. Lodge dedicated the fable-biography of Duke Robert to Thomas Smith, whom he addresses as "the worshipfull and true Mæcenas of learning," one of the few in London who prefer learning to riches. In return for Smith's support, Lodge promises him a work "which shall not only merit and deserue your acceptance, but also mightely profit all such as are studious in all sorts of learning." [1] The moral promise in the address to the "curteous Reader" is that examples in *Robert* will make them eschew the bad and espouse the good.

Lodge lapses into a stiffer, more euphuistic style in *Robert, Duke of Normandy;* it is a harder task, and the results are transparent. The piece opens with a lengthy description of

Duchess Editha, Robert's mother, that is crammed full of the worst of conventional Elizabethan conceits. The passage introduces Editha's tirade to herself because of her barrenness. The curse on Robert stems from her plea: "Well you heauens, since you neglect me, I respect you not, if God vouchsafe me no sonne, the Deuill send me one, so, though my woomb be wretched in bearing, yet happely I shall escape the scandale of vnfruitfulnes." [2] There follows an equally lengthy consolation by Editha's husband that finally results in the birth of Robert amid thunderstorms and earthquakes. Within a brief period in his youth Robert signaled to the world his diabolic heritage; born with teeth, he gave his nurses no little discomfort; and he slit his schoolmaster's throat after poisoning the man's son. A succession of horrible crimes leads to a revenge war and a near mortal wound for Robert.

One of the swiftest reversals in literature takes Robert on a pilgrimage to Rome, where he serves seven years' penance under the guidance of a recluse and finds employment as a court fool. In scandalous abandonment of plot, Lodge has Robert become involved in the romance of the "Souldan" and Emine, the emperor's daughter. Robert proves himself repentant by forestalling the treachery of the Souldan and by stomping his ambassador with something of the fervor of his earlier days. Emine is his reward.

There remains only Robert's reunion in Normandy with his family which transpires as if Robert had been a life-long saint. He rescues his mother from villains who are about to murder her, and the whole tale ends with a moral addressed to the fathers of wayward sons. After the pillage, rapine, and murder of his youth, the reader expects Robert to be set upon by vengeful relatives; but the strength of his conversion tells a powerful story; and at the end he is truly a white knight.

Lodge recognized the value of occasional verse in his prose tales. The device was a success in *Rosalynde*, but the verse of *Robert, Duke of Normandy* makes no comparison with that of *Rosalynde*. The problem lies in the subject: the heavy moral tone of *Robert* does not lend itself well to the bright lyric expression of *Rosalynde*. Robert's confession in "Madrigale" is an example:

> My reasons eye had seene my youthly rage,
>   How it had worne my hopes of vertue bare,
> How carelesse wit was wanton bewties page,
>   And headlesse will true iudgement did insnare,
>   How all was wrackt that hope of wisedome gaue,
>   It wept a world of teares my soule to saue.[3]

Although all the poems are hangovers of Medieval remorse, one, at least, has something of the spirit in sound of the *Rosalynde* poems, and of the *carpe diem* tradition in subject:

> Plucke the fruite and taste the pleasure
>   Youthfull Lordings of delight,
> Whil'st occasion giues you seasure,
>   Feede your fancies and your sight:
>   After death when you are gone,
>   Joy and pleasure is there none.
>
> Here on earth is nothing stable,
>   Fortunes chaunges well are knowne,
> Whil'st as youth doth then enable,
>   Let your seedes of ioy be sowne:
>   After death when you are gone
>   Ioy and pleasure is there none.
>
> Feast it freely with your Louers,
>   Blyth and wanton sweetes doo fade,
> Whilst that louely *Cupid* houers
>   Round about this louely shade:
>   Sport it freelie one to one,
>   After death is pleasure none.
>
> Now the pleasant spring allureth,
>   And both place and time inuites:
> Out alas, what heart endureth
>   To disclaime his sweete delightes?
>   After death when we are gone,
>   Joy and pleasure is there none.[4]

II   Catharos

In the volume containing *Robert, Duke of Normandy*, Lodge published the pamphlet *Catharos: Diogenes in his Singularitie*

that is subtitled *A Nettle for Nice Noses.* Although some of the
mettle of the introduction to the *Rosalynde* appears throughout
the work, the pamphlet on the whole, is mere railing. His
printer, John Bushie, wrote an epistle to Sir John Hart about the
subject: "The matter may at first sight (I graunt) seeme nothing graue, but in the proceeding it will prooue Gratious: *Diogenes* reprooues the vitious, commendes the vertuous, Vnmasks
sinne, and sets downe remedies." [5] Lodge leaves no doubt as to
the moral purpose in the address to the readers, signed Diogenes.

The speakers of the dialogue are Diogenes, Philoplutos, and
Cosmosophos. The reader is reminded of Samuel Daniel's *Musophilus* (1599), in which Musophilus and Philocosmus square
off for a lengthy discussion. Such an arrangement lends itself to
more euphuistic repetitious spouting in *Catharos,* as in Cosmosophos' speech: "There are manie in our Common-weale of
Athens, who haue ripe wits and readie toungs, who if they
catch an inch, will claime an ell; if they put in the finger, will
thrust in the head. . . . If they talke wel, tel them they trip; it
is better smother them in the egge, than smooth with them in
the bird: for the meanest sparrow hath his neb, the lions
whelpe his clawe, the weake thorne his prickle, and the poorest
man his policie. . . ." [6]

Lodge's attack covers wide areas: magistrates, solicitors and
unlettered curates, merchants, and usurers. Once again Lodge
inveighs against those who were so successful in parting him
from his money on the pretense of giving him some. The whole
history of usury, as well as laws opposing it, is paraded for the
reader. After classes of individual sinners, types of sins come
under attack. In the best seven-deadly-sins tradition, luxury
and licentiousness, and all their attendant sins, are discussed—
as well as appropriate remedies for each.

The near connection between Lodge's intent in *Catharos* and
the themes in Spenser's *Shepheardes Calender, Mother Hub-
berd's Tale,* and the Medieval exempla can be seen from this
fable from *Catharos:*

A Hauke called Ormarillus being a stout birde of prey, and seeking
out for a peere, met with a Goshauke, who became his confederate:

these two bold winged rauenors, seeking in the Summer evening for their ordinarie Supper, made this couenant betweene themselues, that whatsoeuer they tooke sould be equally deuided between them: Vpon which conclusion, they both at once seazed vpon a Quaile, and seeing her a little bird too abiect a morcell for their hungrie mawes, they began coulorably to vndermine her, in hope to surprise both her and her young, and courted her in this manner: Choose thee whether (faire bird) thou hadst rather be deuoured alone, or else conducting us to thy chickens and yong ones, to suffer death with them, to satisfie our pleasures. The Quaile being in a quandarie said: Anguish and trouble is falne upon me on euerie side, and what I should do I shunne to doe. Should I loose my yong ones, whom I haue carefully couered in the shell, clocked vnder my wings; whom I haue fed by my toyle, and brought up with much care: no I will not. Lesse hurt is it for mee to die, and to fall into their handes my selfe alone, than to suffer both my selfe and the sillie ones both at once to perish, whereupon without replye shee humbled her to their grype; they greedily deuoured her, and the deuill send them surfets that loue such suppers.[7]

III Euphues Shadow

Catharos shows Lodge's prose in decline; he had lost the talent for neat organization of material as illustrated in *Rosalynde* and he had abandoned his adaptation of Lyly's style for mere imitation of that style. And his next work, *Euphues Shadow* (1592), shows his inspiration in decline. While Lodge was off on his voyage with Cavendish, Greene, who took care of getting his friend's work published, dedicated the book to Robert Ratcliffe, Viscount Fitzwaters, who was, as usual, urged "To be a Mecenas to the well employed laboures of the absent Gentleman."

Lodge himself wrote the brief address, signed "Philautus," preceding the text. The moral tone of the whole is clear; if the lessons *Euphues* taught did not catch on, perhaps the one Philamis teaches will. Lodge must have counted on capturing the remnants—and there could only be remnants in 1592—of Lyly's admirers; he stubbornly sticks to the theme and style of Lyly even though they had long lost popularity. The whole is so like Lyly that, thirteen years after *Euphues,* it must have appeared ridiculous. The hasty preparation for publication may suggest that Lodge wrote *Euphues Shadow* much earlier and, hoping for the impossible, put it suddenly in Greene's hands before his departure. There was only one edition.

There is little Lodge does not borrow from Lyly in the sort of midsummer night's dream mixup among the young people in the tale: Philamis has a friend Philamour; Philamour loves Harpaste; Harpaste, Philamis; and Philamis, "disdainful Eurinome." As the four gather, somewhat like the assemblage in Castiglione's *Book of the Courtier*, they dance and sing to barginets and madrigals, the best of which is Philamis' barginet, one of the finest poems Lodge wrote:

> Happie *Phoebus* in thy flower,
>   On thy teares so sweetly feeding:
>   VVhen she spyeth thy heart bleeding,
> Sorrow dooth hir heart deuoure.
>   Oh that I might Phoebus bee,
>   So my Clitia loved me.
>
> When with glorie thou doost rise,
>   Foorth his fare to showe she putteth
> When in west thy glorie shutteth,
>   Clitia shuts, hir beautie dies.
>   VVere my mistresse such as she,
>   Oh that I might Phoebus be.
>
> Phoebus beautie did allure
>   His faire flower at first to loue him:
> And till time from heauen remooue him,
>   Clitias glorie shall endure.
>   Oh that I might Phoebus bee,
>   So my Clitia loued me.
>
> Thou that houldest in thy hande,
>   Natures glorie, Phoebus treasure:
> Now obserue the selfe same measure,
>   For I burne in selfe same bande.
>   VVere my mistres such as she,
>   Oh that I might Phoebus be.[8]

C. S. Lewis says that in this poem and in "Plucke the fruit" (p. 69) "there is just a hint of that slightly glib, over-emphatic melody which we find in Dryden's songs."[9]

When the soiree settles down in *Euphues Shadow* to a discussion of the question, "Whether it bee better to deserue and haue no friendship, or offend and find fauour," disdainful Eurinome—like a refined Wife of Bath—is first and best in her answer: men must serve women to master them: "for women are like quailes not charmed without sweet call, like Dolphins not allured but by musick, and shew of observance toward them, is best meanes to be soueraignes ouer them. . . . Women admit no porportion, they are peremptorie, theyr choise is as theyr change, and their change as the moon." [10] Philamour's reply is that lovers must thrive on misery for "the more you [women] are praised, the more you repine: the more men serve you, the more you scorne them. . . ." [11]

Had Lodge kept up the courtly lovers' debate, he might have sustained interest, at least in the wit of repartee; but he interrupts this exchange with the entrance of hapless Claetia, who pours out a mournful tale of a lover she had spurned, thereby causing him to take his own life. At the conclusion of her long, rambling confession, she produces her lover's corpse and kills herself. This event sobers the party; and, when the narrative proper resumes, letters are exchanged and then blows are struck among the friends. Philamour wounds Philamis, who disappears in the care of a hermit shepherd; Eurinome goes mad and dies. After much wandering and rediscovery, Philamis and Philamour are reunited; Philamour marries Harpaste; and Philamis becomes a hermit.

The conclusion presents two long sermons, one entitled "Philamis and his Athanatos, containing the deafe man's dialogue":

> Philamis: And what is death?
> Celio: The law of nature, the tribute of the flesh,
> the remedy of euils, the path eyther to heauenly felicity
> or eternall miserie.[12]

The second sermon, much the same, is entitled "Philamis to Anthenor, to comfort him in his exile." It brings the subject back to the beginning: Anthenor was the old counselor who gave advice at the start of the action. Once again the style is euphuistic:

there dwelt at Rauenna (a famous Citie in Italie) a yong Gentleman, who had as great reach in wit as riches, and as many perfec-
tions, as possessions, beautifull hee was, and this was natures benefit: rich he was, and that Fortunes bequest. . . . But as the beast
Varius hath a ritch skin, but a ranke flesh, and the bird Struchio a
big body, but weake wings, so Philamis hauing a rype wit had a
running head, placing his felicitie in trauaile, not in temperance, in
seeking forraine countries, not hearing fruitful counsailes.[13]

Lodge began by inserting poetry in the prose, but the device
did not lend itself as it had in *Rosalynde;* as in the work *Robert,* the moral instruction is too heavy to sustain lyrical inter-
lude, and there is not enough narrative to support such a
change of pace. The old counselor, Anthenor, begins by giving Philamis advice in verse that is far from the lyrics of
Rosalynde:

> The retchlesse race of youths inconstant course,
> (Which weeping age with sorowing teares behoulds)
> Their wretched will (their wofull sorrows source)
> Their wanton wits, their errors manifoldes
> Hath reard my muse, whose springs wan care had dried,
> To name them flie the dangers I haue tried.[14]

Tenney found that Lodge borrowed matter for *Euphues
Shadow* from the anonymous *Dialogues of Creatures moralized*
(1480), and from Girolamo Garimberto's commonplace book
Concetti (1551).[15] On the basis of evidence in *Catharos* and
Euphues Shadow, he believes Lodge was planning a public
avowal of Roman Catholicism just before the Cavendish voyage.[16]

Lodge was desperate before the publication of *Euphues
Shadow.* His literary career, on which he had staked so much,
was floundering; his personal fortunes were ebbing; the future
did not look bright. Perhaps he took the journey with Cavendish to escape from a good many things which were pressing
upon him on all sides, and perhaps he also wrote for the same
reason a plea as an epilogue to *Euphues Shadow:*

Ladies and Gentlemen, I haue posted Philamis from Passan, to
apply his studies in the mountaines of Stiris: if his courting hath

wrought you any content, I doubte not but his contemplations shall yeeld good conceit, he hath layd a line for loftie building, and hath vowed himselfe to great studdie and labour, it only lyes in your fauourable good likings, to make him a forward workman, or to giue ouer in the foundations: the reward he seeks is your acceptance, and fruite you may reape may perhaps prooue science: since therefore all that he requireth is but a good work for a great worke, vouchsafe him that which lieth in you to bestow, and in him to deserue, and till that time, farewell.[17]

Thomas Lodge had not yet made a connection with his age. He had published with confidence, as in *Rosalynde;* he had written in hope, as in the *Wounds of Civil War* and in *Euphues Shadow;* he had written a "first" in *Scillaes Metamorphosis;* yet all this variety failed to please the Elizabethan reader.

IV *The Cavendish Voyage*

Thomas Lodge was never blessed with good fortune, and it seeemed his lot to fall in with one of fortune's outcasts, Sir Thomas Cavendish. If ever a sea-adventure was planned to curb young would-be sailors' desires, it was Cavendish's. Not one shred of romance of the Elizabethan buccaneers touched his expedition; he was blighted from the beginning of this voyage, after successfully circumnavigating the globe in 1586–88. This great success made him the hero of the moment in England, where ballads of his conquests were sung in his honor. After the glowing accounts of his first voyage, a good many young men must have been anxious to buy a place on the second, and Lodge must have considered himself fortunate to secure one. The Canaries trip had brought him the success of *Rosalynde,* and a second adventure with a renowned privateer might also bring success.

Tenney has assembled the principal accounts of the second Cavendish voyage out of publications of the Hakluyt Society,[18] and the story of infamy and death is now well known. Disaster followed disaster until the expedition, its ships scattered, its crew in mutiny, and its leader losing the grip of command, split apart after attempting to pass through the Straits of Magellan. Cavendish, a broken man, died in 1592 and was buried at sea. Lodge probably returned with the flagship a year later, but he had no kind words for Cavendish in a reference to the voyage in the preface to *A Margarite of America:* "Som foure yeres being at sea with M. Candish [Cavendish] (whose memorie if I repent not, I lament not). . . ." [19] Indeed, the happiest and most profitable part of the voyage for Lodge was his brief stay at Santos, in Brazil. Otherwise, his wounded fortunes gained nothing from the disaster, since the little prizes the expedition had taken were demanded by the Crown. Lodge was again penniless in London.

Although we have already noted that at some indeterminate date Lodge became a Roman Catholic, his writings after *Rosalynde,* whether written earlier or not, show a marked influence of Lodge's serious readings in Catholic literature,[20] and of an attempt to settle moral and religious questions. And Catholicism in Elizabethan England, added to his ill-success as a writer and as an adventurer, results in nothing but despair. But we must add even more misfortune—his family.

At the death of his parents, as noted above, Thomas' brother William had become executor of the estate; moreover, Lady Lodge had left a legacy for Thomas in William's care. When Thomas arrived in London after the voyage, he turned to William for help. William, so like Saladyne of *Rosalynde,* refused; and, according to Thomas, William also sent men to beat his brother while en route to London. When Thomas sued William for assault, an almost comic exchange of suits and countersuits followed, outlined in some detail by Sisson.[21] The final disposition of the Star Chamber was that Thomas should receive two hundred pounds from William.

V William Longbeard *and* Phillis

From 1593 to 1596 Lodge must have been making a final decision: one last attempt would be made to capture the literary eye of London readers. He published rapidly a series of miscellaneous writings. The first of these was a group of short histories entitled *The Life and Death of William Longbeard.*

References in the preface of the work addressed to the readers indicate that Lodge was weary of the reading public's taste, as he had been earlier when writing *Scillaes Metamorphosis*. He echoes the current criticisms of many writers that "new fasions" destroy good style, and worth is no longer appreciated: "Taylors and writers nowadaies are in like estimate, if they want new fasions they are not fansied: and if the stile be not of the new stamp, tut the Author is a foole. . . ." [22] Tenney thinks the address is particularly directed to Thomas Nashe as a reply to a supposed Nashe attack in his *Pierce Penilesse* on Lodge, [23] but Paradise argues convincingly that the Nashe portrait is too general to have much relation to Lodge. [24]

The histories in the *Longbeard* volume are "pure hack work," as Paradise says. [25] They are aimed at the vast interest Elizabethans had in their own past, and in general histories such as Raphael Holinshed's *Chronicles of England* and William Warner's *Albion's England*. Besides the Longbeard story, there are eleven other histories, most of them brief, running not much over two pages. The reader will find a marked difference between the style of Lodge's prose in *Euphues Shadow* and in this "new" fashion. A certain directness and succinctness make the narratives more lively and interesting. While euphuistic passages still occur, tempered as always by Lodge's control, they are rarer.

After *Longbeard* Lodge abandoned prose, and not until he wrote *Margarite of America* in 1596 did he again attempt narrative. His next efforts were exclusively with poetry, and resulted in the publication of *Phillis: honoured with pastorall sonnets, elegies, and amorous delights*. Many of these poems were translations and paraphrases, which have dutifully been traced to their sources by a number of scholars. [26]

The rage for sonneteering began with Sir Philip Sidney's *Astrophel and Stella* in 1591. Samuel Daniels' *Delia* followed in 1592, as well as Henry Constable's *Diana*. Lodge, always ready to try a new thing, published *Phillis* in 1593; and he dedicated it to another on his growing list of Maecenases, the Countess of Shrewsbury, "the Soueraigne and shee Mecaenas of my toyle," encouraging her "to looke and like of homlie Phillis in her Country caroling, and to countenance her poore and affectionate Sheepheard, who promiseth vnder the only encouragement of so noble a Lady, to employ all his best deseignes, life, and studies, to your good lyking." [27]

A number of interesting references appear in the "Induction," which precedes the forty sonnets in the cycle. The opening line, "I that obscur'd haue fled the Sceane of Fame," is a curiously perceptive glance by Lodge at his own career. Lines 7–12 seem to refer to Sidney, Daniel, and perhaps Spenser as sonnet writers:

> Oh you high sp'rited Paragons of witte,
> That flye to fame beyond our earthly pitch,
> Whose sence is sound, whose words are feat and fitte,
> Able to make the coyest eare to itch:
> Shroud with your mighty wings that mount so well,
> These little loues, new crept from out the shell.[28]

He makes specific reference to Spenser and Daniel later:

> If so you come where learned Colin feedes
> His louely flocke, packe thence and quickly haste you;
> You are but mistes before so bright a sunne,
> Who hath the Palme for deepe inuention wunne,[29]

and,

> Kisse Delias hand for her sweet Prophets sake,
> VVhose not affected but well couched teares:
> Haue power, haue worth, a Marble minde to shake;
> Whose fame, no Iron-age or time out weares.[30]

Phillis is made up of forty sonnets and a number of short lyrics, eclogues, and elegies. Some of the lyrics are among Lodge's best poetry; a few of these had been printed earlier in the *Phoenix Nest* (1585). Not all of the sonnets are in the strict form we have become familiar with. One of the earliest adapters of Italian models to English was Thomas Watson, who published a number of imitations and translations in his Ἑκατομπαθία, or *Passionate Century of Love*, in 1582. The one hundred poems are eighteen-line sonnets inspired by a variety of Continental writers, most of them prefaced by a prose note indicating theme and source. The familiar fourteen-line sonnet, while popular, was not the exclusive form; and, as we have seen before, Lodge and others experimented with sonnets of varying length and meters. His Sonnet XIII is not unlike the lyrics of *Rosalynde:*

> Loue guides the roses of thy lippes,
> And flies about them like a bee.
> If I approch he forward skippes,
> And if I kisse he stingeth me.
> Loue in thine eyes doth build his bower,
> And sleepes within their prettie shine:
> And if I looke the boy will lower,
> And from their orbes shootes shaftes deuine.
> Loue workes thy heart within his fire,
> And in my teares doth firm the same:
> And if I tempt it will retire,
> And of my plaintes doth make a game.
> Loue let me cull his choycest flowers,
> And pittie me, and calme hir eye,
> Make soft hir heart, dissolue hir lowers,
> Then will I praise thy dietie.
> But if thou do not loue, Ile trulye serue hir,
> In spight of thee, by firme faith deserue hir.[31]

Not so successful is Sonnet XXXVII, fourteen lines of hexameters, beginning: "These fierce incessant waues that streame along my face." [32]

Most of the sonnets are fourteen lines of three quatrains and a couplet, or what is called Shakespearian. None of them is outstanding, as a few of Shakespeare's, Daniel's, and Sidney's are; but almost all of Lodge's have that musical ease typical of Elizabethan song and poetry and that is so remarkable in the 1580's after the earlier attempts of John Skelton, Alexander Barclay, Barnabe Googe, or of the *Mirror for Magistrates.* Many of Lodge's are pure pleasure, if not great, like Sonnet III, one of best in statement and structure:

> In fancies world an Atlas haue I beene,
> Where yet the Chaos of my ceaseless care:

Is by hir eies vnpitied and vnseene,
In whom all giftes but pity planted are . . .[33]

Or Sonnet XI,

My fraile and earthly barke, by reasons guide,
Which holds the helme, whilst wil doth weilde the saile,[34]

Or Sonnet XXIII,

Burst burst poore heart thou hast no longer hope,
Captiue mine eyes vnto eternall sleepe,
Let all my sences have no further scope,
Let death be lord of me and all my sheepe . . .[35]

C. S. Lewis remarks on the immediacy of Lodge's Classical al-
lusions that removes the encyclopedic learning from his poetry.[36] Sonnets XXXIII and XXXIV, though in some ways cata-
logues, are nevertheless local and charming; moreover, they
show what Lewis means:

The warriour Mars, bequeath'd her fierce disdaine,
Venus her smile, and Phoebe all her fayre . . .

I would in rich and golden coloured raine,
With tempting showers in pleasant sort descend,
Into faire Phillis lappe . . .
I would be changed to a milk-white Bull
When midst the gladsome fieldes he should appeare . . .
I were content to wearie out my paine,
To bee Narcissus so she were a spring. . . .[37]

Following Sonnet XX are two eclogues and an elegy which
help to establish the pastoral setting of the cycle. In the first
eclogue, Demades and Damon discuss in traditional terms the
problems of love much as Colin and his cronies do in Spenser's
Shepheardes Calender. The verse is Lodge's standard, the six-
line stanza. The second eclogue is an interesting innovation in
trochaic tetrameter quatrains:

> Muses helpe me, sorrow swarmeth,
> Eyes are fraught with seas of languish:
> Heauie hope my solace harmeth,
> Mindes repast is bitter anguish. . . .[38]

Despite the tiresome repetition in meter, the compact expression is a refreshing change. But the elegy, a lover's lament abounding in general statements, does nothing for Lodge's credit as a poet.

The cycle concludes with an ode, one of Lodge's most familiar poems, first printed in the 1585 *Phoenix Nest:*

> Nowe I find thy lookes were fained,
> Quickly lost, and quicklie gained:
> Soft thy skinne, like wool of Weathers,
> Hart vnstable, light as feathers.
> Tongue vntrustie, subtil sighted,
> Wanton will, with change delighted.
> Siren pleasant, foe to reason
> Cupid plague thee for this treason.
>
> Of thine eyes, I made my mirror,
> From thy beautie came my error,
> All thy words I counted wittie,
> All thy smiles I deemed pitty.
> Thy false teares that me agrieued,
> First of all my trust deceiued.
> Siren pleasant, foe to reason
> Cupid plague thee for this treason.
>
> Faind acceptance when I asked,
> Louely words with cunning masked,
> Holy vowes but hart vnholly,
> Wretched man my trust was folly:
> Lillie white and prettie winking,
> Sollemne vowes, but sorry thinking.
> Siren pleasant, foe to reason
> Cupid plague thee for this treason.
>
> Now I see O seemely cruell,
> Others warme them at my fuell,

Wil shall guide me in this durance,
Since in loue is no assurance.
Change thy pasture, take thy pleasures
Beautie is a fading treasure.
Siren pleasant, foe to reason
Cupid plague thee for this treason.

Prime youth lusts not age still follow
And make white these tresses yellow,
Wrinckled face for lookes delightfull,
Shall acquaint the Dame despightfull:
And when time shall eate thy glory,
Then too late thou wilt be sorry.
Siren pleasant, foe to reason
Cupid plague thee for this treason.[39]

A certain musical delight emerges from the rapidity of the octosyllabic couplets and especially from the abundance of feminine rhymes. Lodge was at home with this kind of verse.

Appended to the *Phillis* cycle is a long Medieval lament that takes us back once more to the *Mirror for Magistrates*, for Lodge's *The Complaint of Elstred* sounds much like *Shore's Wife* in the *Mirror*. The verse is Lodge's six-line stanza, and he announces at the beginning that the poem is a "wofull vision." John Higgin's contributions to the *Mirror* (fifth edition, 1574) began with four pieces—the histories of King Albanact, son of Brutus; King Humber; King Locrinus; and Queen Elstred and Lady Sabrine. From these tales, particularly the last two, Lodge got the story of the *Complaint*. So in tone, style, and subject Lodge was indebted to the *Mirror*, one of Elizabethan England's most popular productions.

Lodge wrote several short lyrics for the miscellanies. These—like the lyrics in *Rosalynde, Phillis*, and *A Margarite of America*—are excellent song-like poems. We notice Lodge's versatile, smooth handling of cadences, a flexibility which few of his contemporaries had:

Striue no more,
  Forsaken ioyes to spring:
Since care hath clipt thy wing:
  But stoope those lampes before:

> That nurst thee vp at first, with friendly smiles,
> And now through scornes thy trust beguiles.
>
>   Pine away,
> That pining you may please;
> For death betides you ease:
>   Oh sweete and kinde decay;
> To pine and die, whilst Loue giues looking on,
> And pines to see you pining mone.
>
>   Dying ioyes,
> Your shrine is constant hart,
> That glories in his smart:
>   Your Trophies are anoyes,
> And on your tombe, by Loue these lines are plaste,
> Loe heere they lie, whom scorne defaste.[40]

Most of the *Phoenix Nest* poems are lovers' complaints in the usual vein. The best are non-traditional forms, in which Lodge strives for sound effects through short lines as in,

> My bonnie Lasse thine eie,
>   So slie,
> Hath made me sorrowe so:
> Thy Crimsen cheekes my deere,
>   So cleere,
> Haue so much wrought my woe . . .[41]

Two poems were printed in *England's Helicon* (1600), probably written long before 1595, when Lodge gave up writing poetry. The first is a pastoral, praising the country life:

> Carelesse vvorldlings, outrage quelleth
>   All the pride and pompe of Cittie:
> But true peace with Sheepheards dwelleth,
>   (Sheepheards who delight in pittie). . . .[42]

The second is a short lyric narrative of Cupid and Venus:

> In pride of youth, in midst of May,
> When birds with many a merry lay,
>   salute the Sunnes vp-rising

> I sate me downe fast by a Spring,
> And while these merry Chaunters sing,
>   I fell vpon surmizing. . . .[43]

The wounds of love, so easy to find, so hard to endure, lead the poet to this conclusion, after a succinct narrative illustrating the point:

> She suckt the wound, and swag'd the sting,
> And little Loue ycurde did sing,
>   then let no Louer sorrow:
> To day though greefe attaint his hart,
> Let him with courage bide the smart,
>   amends will come tomorrow.[44]

In summary, the years from 1591–94 were not successful for Lodge; they mark the lowest point in these middle years of his career. The literary productions were unsuccessful among English readers, the sea voyage was abortive, and he was in trouble with his family over his inheritance. Once again he had to find a new avenue; but, before he started on it, he took one last bow to the literary world.

CHAPTER 5

Farewell to Writing

WHEN Lodge's final volume of poetry was published in 1595, he was prepared to sink or swim as a writer; and he apparently feared he would sink. *A Fig for Momus: containing pleasant varietie, included in Satyres, Eclogues, and Epistles* incorporates in its title a warning to carping critics. The attack in the introductory letter is directed, "in despight of the detractor," to those "Who worthely deseruing the name of Momus, shall rather at my hands haue a figge to choake him, then hee, and his lewd tongue shall haue a frumpe to check me: Sheepe are soonest wooried by curdogs, because they are mild: but hee that nips him soundly, that bites him cowardly, purchaseth his owne peace, and escapes much perill." [1] He then explains the title and the purpose of his poems as, "vnder this title I have thought good to include Satyres, Eclogues, and Epistles: first by reason that I studie to delight with varietie, next because I would write in that forme, wherein no man might chalenge me with seruile imitation, (wherewith heretofore I haue been vniustlie taxed)." [2] He promises a whole *Centon* of satires if these please, and he commends his eclogues "to men of approued iudgement, whose margents though I fill not with quotations, yet their matter, and handling, will show my diligence. . . ."

Of his epistles, he says that "they are in that kind, wherein no Englishman of our time hath publiquely written . . .": "Briefly, I haue so written, as I haue read: so read, as I can iudge: In which respect, if any man doubt, let him aske and I will resolue him: if any man reprooue, let him looke to it, I will nip him: for as I am readie to satisfie the reasonable, so I haue a gird in store for a Railer." [3]

I *The Satires*

The Satires of *A Fig for Momus* are among the first imitations of Roman satire in England, and Lodge was the first to print satires in this genre. Joseph Hall published his collection of satires, *Virgidemiae*, in 1597 and Donne was writing his satires during 1594–97, but these were not published until later. A good number of Englishmen had written satire: Chaucer, Langland, Skelton, and Spenser were forerunners; but none of these attempted to imitate the form of Latin satire. Horace, Juvenal, and Persius were known to Chaucer and Langland, but only through secondhand sources. Skelton knew the Roman satirists better, and after the humanists exerted their influence in the universities, Latin satire must have been favorite reading material.

Roman satirists followed the model of Lucilius, and *Satura Luciliana* was distinguished from other types of satire by exclusive use of verse—especially dactylic hexameter—in form, and much variety in subject. One of the most common subjects for satire—Classical or Renaissance—is that the world is "going to the dogs": Juvenal and Persius exposed the vices of their fellow Romans, and the English Renaissance satirists imitated the pattern in exposing the follies of English life, as Lodge states in this couplet: "And cunning sinne being clad in Vertues shape / Flies much reproofe, and many scornes doth scape." [4]

Lodge's debt to the Roman satirists is everywhere evident. His Satire 3 [5] is modeled closely on Juvenal's Satire XIV. The subject—evil influences of parents on children—was popular in the Classical and Renaissance periods; Quintilian's *Institutes* treats the problem, and Ben Jonson's *Everyman in his Humor* contains a passage on the subject. Lodge's paraphrase of Juvenal is shown in this passage:

> And where the mind is willing and addict,
> Th'examples are more forcible and strict:
> And though some natures, by especiall grace
> Correct themselues, and giue not follie place,
> Yet lean the most part, to example so,
> That what they like, they hardlie can forgoe.
> Then (gentle friend) from damned deeds abstaine,

> From lawles ryots, and from pleasures vaine,
> If not regarding of thine owne degree,
> Yet in behalfe of thy posteritie:
> For we are docible to imitate,
> Depraued pleasures tho degenerate.[6]

The parallel passage in Juvenal illustrates how much Lodge followed Satire XIV:

sic natura iubet: velocius et citius nos corrumpunt vitiorum exempla domestica, magnis cum subeant animos auctoribus. unus et alter forsitan haec spernant iuvenes, quibus arte benigna et meliore luto finxit praecordia Titan, sed relinquos fugienda patrum vestigia ducunt et monstrata diu veteris trahit orbita culpae.

Abstineas igitur damnandis. huius enim vel una potens ratio est, ne crimina nostra sequantur ex nobis geniti, quoniam dociles imitandis turpibus ac pravis omnes sumus. . . .[7]

Thus Nature orders: we are more quickly and rapidly corrupted by evils at home, since they enter our minds on great authority. One or another youth —created by better light and art —may perhaps avoid these evils, but the rest are led by parents' steps which they should flee, and are drawn into the old circle of vice which has been shown them for a long time. Therefore, abstain from practices which must be condemned for this one overwhelming reason: that our crimes not be imitated by our children, for we can all be taught what is evil and depraved. . . .

In all, some sixty-three lines of Juvenal's Satire XIV find their way into Lodge's one hundred and four lines.

The opening lines of Lodge's Satire 5 also show inspiration from Juvenal: "In every land from Gades to Ganges flood / Too few they be that think vpon their good: / Too few that by discretion can discerne / What profit rightly doth themselues concerne."[8] Juvenal's Satire X reads: "Omnibus in terris, quae sunt a Gadibus usque / Auroram et Gangen, pauci dinoscere possunt / vera bona atque illis multum diversa, remota / erroris nebula. . . ."[9] (In all lands from Gades to Ganges and the Dawn, there are few who can distinguish true good from its many opposites, removing the clouds of error.) And these lines, also from Lodge's Satire 5, echo the famous lines in Horace's Satires II, vi:

An humble cote entapissed with mosse,
A lowlie life that feares no sodaine losse:
A mind that dreads no fal, nor craues no crowne,
But makes his true-content, his best renowne:
These are the choice contents, the goods, the gaine,
Which rightly can be ours: the rest are vain.

(5, ll. 71–76, p. 50)

Horace, in the famous lines from II, vi, says: "Hoc erat in votis:
modus agri non ita magnus, / hortus ubi et tecto vicinus iugis
aquae fons / et paulum silvae super his foret." [10] (This was my
prayer: a humble farm, not very large, a garden, a fountain of
water, and somewhat beyond these, a little woods. . . .)

Lodge followed his Roman masters not only in spirit, but
also in form, adapting the dactylic hexameters to the more
comfortable iambic pentamenter couplet, a distinguishing
mark from his time on of English verse satire. Lodge's couplets
are smooth and urbane, as though he wrote from long experience with the form: "All men are willing with the world to
haulte [limp] / But no man takes delight to know his fault." His
verse form is best in such sweeping generalizations as: "T'is
better be a foole then be a fox; / For Folly is rewarded and
respected, / Where subtiltie is hated and reiected."

The subjects of the satires are as diverse as Horace's and Juvenal's, ranging from the folly of his fellow man in general to
the vices of avarice and the evils of ambition in particular. A
number of "types" are described under the "names of certaine
Romaines," as this one in Satire 1:

Tell blear-eied Linus that his sight is cleere,
Heel pawne himselfe, to buy thee bread and beere:
But tuch me Quintus with his stincking breath,
The dastard will defie thee to the death.

(ll. 43–46, p. 11)

He concludes the satire with a generalization:

Thus with the world, the world dissembles still,
And to their own confusions follow ill;

> Houlding it true felicitie to flie,
> Not from the sinne, but from the seeing eie. . . .
> (ll. 71–74, p. 12)

Lodge's picture of the despicable, miserly old man in Satire 4 has a number of companion portraits in literature; he may have borrowed the idea for his covetous man from Juvenal's Satire IV, which presents a devastating picture of a miser (lines 119–88). Persius' Satire IV describes a miser who eats onions and drinks vinegar for his lunch to conserve grocery stocks; he is not only stingy in his diet, but he is also a thoroughly unlovely character, broken with age, as in Lodge:

> Looke on thy selfe, age hath thee by the backe,
> Thy haires are white, which erst were frisseld black:
> Thine eies are suncke, thy cheeks are leane and pale,
> Thy lips are blew, thy breath is stincking stale,
> Thy grinders gone, thy ghastlie gout, and murre
> Do breake thy sleepes, and scarcely let thee sturre:
> Thy memorie is dul, and wel nie dead,
> Thy tongue alreadie faulters in thy head.[11]

Lodge's views on the vanity of human wishes are like those of Sir Thomas Wyatt in the letter to John Poins on the courtier's life. The vanity of ambition, of too much striving, is summarized in these lines from Satire 5: "Who builds on strength by policie is stript: / Who trusts his wit, by wit is soonest tript" (ll. 33–34, p. 49).

Lodge's Satires are witty in subject and polished in form; he gave his readers their first experience with Roman styles in English satire, beginning a trend which remained popular through the ages of Dryden and Pope.

II *The Epistles*

The epistles of *A Fig for Momus* are indeed "that kind, wherein no Englishman of our time hath publiquely written." As Lodge borrowed form and style from the Romans for his satires, so he borrowed for his epistles, the difference lying in name only. The best of Lodge's epistles concern Renaissance pseudo-science: Epistle 2 on dreams, Epistle 7 on alchemy, and Epistle 3 on overweight.

Lodge assembled all the accepted physiological and astrological explanations for dreams in Epistle 2.[12] Two major physiological causes for dreams were the physical and mental condition of the dreamer, governed largely by the "humors" generated in the body, as we knew long ago from Pertelote in Chaucer's *Nun's Priests Tale*. Lodge states: "For when as choler swarmes in breast or hed, / Men dreame of things inflam'd and fierie red, / And whereas fleugme preuailes, abounds and springs, / We dreame of watrie, colde and frostie things." (ll. 45–48). The astrological causes for dreams come from angelic or diabolic spirits, often through the vehicle of the stars: "For so the staid star-gazers doe areede, / That from celestial bodies do proceede / The course and workings of our dreames in sleepe" (ll. 39–41).

In Epistle 7, Lodge castigates the abusers of alchemy—like his predecessors, Petrarch, Chaucer, Erasmus, Cornelius Agrippa, and his successor, Ben Jonson—in a tradition that goes far back in literature. The hue and cry against alchemy shows how widespread interest in the pseudo-science was. Lodge bases his invective against these charlatans who promise much but produce little on James Sandford's translation of Agrippa's *De Incertitudine et Vanitate scientiarum*.[13]

The third epistle, directed to Mistress Anne Lodge, his niece,[14] is the most modern in subject—how to lose weight: "You pray me to aduise, and tell you what / Will take away your pursines and fat." [15] A good deal of medical lore precedes the cure, which is timeless:

> Watch much, and sleeping little, hardly lie:
> Walke much, and tosse, and tumble in the sunne,
> Delight to ride, to hauke, to hunt, to runne,
> Drinke little, gargarize, flie grosser food.
>   (ll. 114–17, p. 56)

But all the advice cannot cap the closing "why bother" lines: ". . . for fat, slicke, faire, and full / Is better lik't then leane, lancke, spare, and dull" (ll. 133–34, p. 57).

The remaining epistles are of varying interest. Epistle 1 is dedicated to Momus, and Tenney thinks it is a type of school exercise Lodge may have written at Oxford,[16] one not unlike Milton's *Prolusions;* for it is heavily indebted to the unnatural natural history of Pliny and to a host of other Classical writers. The interesting part of the epistle is not Lodge's catalogue of Classical rain and storm signs, but the reasons behind the signs, which must be explained with Medieval sureness to that "dull dunce," Momus:

> How proue you that, cries *Momus* once againe?
> Why thus dull dunce: The moyst and stormie time
> Fitting the frogges, that dwell in wette and slime,
> Makes them by naturall instinct to croke,
> Because ensuing raines the spleene prouoke.[17]

Epistles 5 and 6 have some literary interest. Epistle 5 is dedicated to Michael Drayton, after he had seen that poet's *Endymion and Phoebe,* and discusses "learned nines and threes" in compliment to Drayton's numerological passage in *Endymion.* In an introductory passage, Lodge discusses the present state of poetry and holds out the hope that good poets and good poetry will succeed:

> So poetrie restraind in errors bounds,
> With poisoned words, and sinful sweetnes wounds,
> But clothing vertue, and adorning it,
> Wit shines in vertue, vertue shines in wit.[18]

Epistle 6, "In Praise of his Mistris Dogge," caused him a gibe from another contemporary, John Marston, in his *Scourge of Villainy* (1599). Lodge begins the epistle:

> Madam, my Muse wing'd by your kind request,
> To praise a dog hath solemnly profest,
> And for reward, desires no further grace,
> Than for a night to grant me Pretties place.
>
> (ll. 1–4)

Walker has noted how closely Marston imitated Lodge in satirizing fops who fawn on their mistresses' pets, and attacks Lodge under the name of Phrigio:

> But, out on Phrigio
> That wish'd he were his mistress' dog, to go
> And lick her milk-white fist! O pretty grace!
> That pretty Phrigio begs but Prettys place.[19]

III   *The Eclogues*

Unlike the satires and epistles of *A Fig for Momus*, the satiric eclogues of Lodge offer nothing new in form since the pastoral had already been established in English letters. Alexander Barclay and Barnabe Googe had published eclogues on Classical models, George Turberville published a translation of Mantuan's eclogues in 1567, Spenser's *Shepheardes Calender* appeared in 1579, and in 1593 Michael Drayton published his *Shepherd's Garland Fashion'd in Nine Eglogs*.

Lodge's Eclogue 1 is addressed to Spenser as Colin, and follows the idea of "February" in the *Shepheardes Calender*. The long fable in Lodge's "Cantus" is similar to the oak and briar fable of the "February" eclogue: both are moral tales told by "natural" characters, and both contain traditional arguments between youth and age.

Eclogue 3, addressed to Drayton as Rowland, continues the theme of the first eclogue, but is more personal. Lodge uses his literary name, Golde, which Drayton had given him in *Endymion and Phoebe*:

> And thou my Goldey, which in Sommer days
> Hast feasted us with merry roundelays
> And when my Muse scarce able was to fly
> Didst imp her wings with thy sweete Poesie.[20]

Lodge argues that patrons "skantle learning with a seruile pay," and dedicate themselves to personal gain instead of patronage of the arts, a situation poets and artists had decried for centuries. Theocritus had found the same situation, and

Lodge's contemporary Samuel Daniel wrote at length of the problem in his *Musophilus* (1599).[21]

In Eclogues 2 and 4 Lodge returns to an old theme, the youth-age debate. These lack, however, the autobiographical references which make Eclogues 1 and 3 interesting. W. W. Greg's judgment that all the eclogues "are serious, even weighty . . . and befit the mood of the poet who first sought to acclimatize the classical satire" and that they do not "testify to any high poetic gift" summarizes their value and shortcomings.[22]

Lodge tossed the fig to Momus; unfortunately it did not choke that carping critic: the satires, epistles, and eclogues of *A Fig for Momus* were received unkindly, and Lodge prepared to end his literary career. In the next year, 1596, he got all his writings ready for publication and gave them to his publishers. In doing so, he prepared also his farewell to literature.

IV A Margarite of America

The first of these last works is *A Margarite of America,* a prose romance, and the nearest thing to a novel in the modern sense that Lodge wrote. Sir Edmund Gosse called it "one of the prettiest of histories," [23] and other critics have praised the romance highly. Baker deems it to be Lodge's "best romance . . . [one] evidently modelled on the heroical parts of the *Arcadia,* but with a tragic instead of a happy conclusion." [24] C. S. Lewis, who also deems it Lodge's best romance, thinks it is closer to Heliodorus and Sidney than other romances, but "harsher and (in some ways) more splendid than either." [25] "If the book is not realistic, it is real; the compulsive imagination of a larger, brighter, bitterer, more dangerous world than ours." [26] The harsh and splendid aspects of *A Margarite* are not unlike the same aspects in Jacobean tragedy.

In the dedication, Lodge tells the readers where he wrote it: "Touching the place where I wrote this, it was in those straits christned by *Magelan* . . . so that as there was great wonder in the place wherein I writ this, so likewise might it be maruelled, that in such scanty fare, such causes of feare, so mightie discouragements, and many crosses, I should deserue or eternize anything." [27] The griefs of the Cavendish voyage were still with him, but he was apparently well-off financially on the "4. of Maie 1596," for he dates A Margarite "From my house."

The address to the "Gentlemen Readers" contains biographical data about the Cavendish voyage in which Lodge tells us there was an original version of the work in Spanish, from which he wrote; but Lodge was no doubt using an old, conventional device—such as Chaucer had with his Lollius. Underhill says "the statement of Lodge cannot be understood to apply further than to the design of his story." [28] The whole situation surrounding the writing is indicative of the voyage and of Lodge's attitude at the time:

The place where I began my worke, was a ship, where many souldiers of good reckning finding disturbed stomackes; it can not but stand with your discretion to pardon an vndiscreete and vnstaied penne, for hands may vary where stomacks miscary. The time I wrote in, was when I had rather will to get my dinner, then to win my fame. The order I wrote in, was past order, where I rather obserued mens hands lest they sould strike me, then curious reason of men to condemne mee. In a worde, I wrote vnder hope rather the fish should eate both me writing, and my paper written, then fame should knowe me, hope sould acquaint her with me, or any but miserie should heare mine ending.[29]

A number of elements from Lodge's earlier prose works are evident in A Margarite of America: the cruelty of Robert, Duke of Normandy, and the adventures of William Longbeard; the lion episode with Saladyne in Rosalynde; the mixed-up lovers of Euphues Shadow; and, of course, the remnants of euphuism in style. But the style is more like that in William Longbeard: an attempt at direct, concise prose narrative. But some of the old euphuistic style is there: ". . . let vs haue an eie to Cusco and the emperour thereof, who no sooner arriued in his court, but like the good gardner, knowing his times to plant; like the fortunate husband well trained to yoake and plough, learned of Trisolium, who lifteth vp her leaues against tempest; and the emet, who by her prouision and trauel foretelleth a showre and trouble that followeth, thought good. . . ." [30] And there are a number of passages in which

characters declaim to themselves at great lengths and vehe-
mence on fortune, grief, love, happiness, or whatever, as we
have seen in *Forbonius and Prisceria* and *Rosalynde*.

The story tells of the union of two countries through the marriage of Margarita of Mosco and Arsadachus of Cusco. Arsadachus, a villain, soon reveals his character at the Moscan court
through deceit and murder, but he escapes to Cusco without
punishment. Margarita follows him, aided by an old counselor,
Arsinous, who is seeking revenge, and a friendly lion. Arsadachus spurns Margarita, marries another, and laughs at the
death of his parents. He finally becomes insane, murdering his
new wife, his son, and Margarita. In a lucid moment he realizes
his crimes, blinds himself, and takes his own life.

The elements of magic in *Margarite* are new. Margarita and
her lion remind the reader of Una and the lion in *The Faerie
Queene* (I, iii), and Arsinous is a sort of Merlin who avenges
the multiple crimes of Arsadachus with a magic box. Most striking, however, are the chains of events which attempt to make
the narrative realistic and the characters "develop." Lodge does
not spend any time on motivation: the characters, as in most
Renaissance narrative, are impelled by outside and unex-
plained forces. But in Arsadachus' deception, in Margarita's
grief, and in Arsinous' revenge, are seeds of a good story. The
Senecan bloodiness at the end is dramatic reality which Elizabethans were demanding on the stage.

Lodge writes swift narrative in some passages. The havoc
around Minecius and Philenia's deaths is told with dispatch
and energy, and the ending is equally swift and concrete. Had
Lodge chosen to write more narratives, he would have attained
the realistic touches of a Defoe.

Although *A Fig for Momus* was Lodge's last poetic endeavor, he published a number of lyrics in *Margarite*. None of
them approaches the quality of the lyrics in *Rosalynde*, but
Margarite is not an Arcadian romance. Among the lyrics worth
attention is the "Ages of Man" embroidered in the decor of
Protomachus' room:

> Thus life in name is but a death in beeing,
> A burthen to the soule by earth intangled:

Then put thou off that vaile that lets thy seeing,
O wretched man with many torments mangled,
Since neither childe, nor youth, nor staid, nor aged,
The stormes of wretched life may be asswaged.[31]

In some instances, Lodge credits his borrowings. The two "Pietati" are translations of the Italian poet Dolce; but, in most cases, Lodge translates or paraphrases more freely. Gosse notes that "with Ganimede now ioines the shining sun" is the earliest appearance of the sestina in English literature.[32] A good many sonnets are sprinkled through the text, some of them excellent, as "When as my pale to her pure lips united," and "Twixt reuerence and desire, how am I vexed."

V The Diuel Coniured

Some of the writings Lodge published in 1596 had not been published earlier because of the subject matter. As early as his Oxford days there were indications of Lodge's interest in Catholicism, and, as we have seen, he finally joined the Roman Church. In some of his earlier works, notably in *Robert, Duke of Normandy* and in *Catharos,* he expresses interest in the contemplative, dedicated life which comes after a change in attitude. In the next three pamphlets following publication of *Margarite,* this interest becomes more obvious. The first, *The Diuel Coniured,* again employs the device of a hermit, a recluse, who directs and straightens the thinking of detractors to the point that they follow his way of life. Anthony, the hermit in *The Diuel Coniured,* persuades three young men that their philosophies are wrong and that they must follow the holy, ascetic life. Lodge writes with great warmth and sincerity in the first few pages, before he discusses the types and influences of devils loose in the world. The bulk of the treatise answers Asterius, a magician, on the question of devils and supernatural powers. Anthony condemns the study of astrology and necromancy, but reassures his listeners that devils are about, preying especially on women, who are easy targets.

The work is dedicated with some bravado to John Fortescue, chancellor of the exchequer and member of the Queen's Privy Council; but in the epistle to "gentlemen readers" Lodge expresses one wish: "I had rather you should now condemn me for default in Retoricke, then as in times past, commend my stile, and lament my iudgement." [33] The style is improved; there is less euphuism and more direct prose, as in the short pieces of *William Longbeard* and in some passages in *Margarite*. Much of the discourse is in this vein: "The solitary man (I tell thee) liuing on the earth, forsaketh the same, and mortified in the flesh, is planted in heauen by the spirit, he burneth in the loue of God, to banish the loue of this world." [34]

VI   Wits Misery

The second of these pamphlets, *Wits Misery, or the Worlds Madness,* a Renaissance treatment of the seven deadly sins, is the most readable treatise Lodge wrote. The style, purged of euphuism, has the grace and smoothness of the best of the seventeenth-century prose writers. To this improvement, Lodge added that singular ability of his to make the old new. The seven sins he discusses have nothing of the traditional quality aside from name: they are not the sins that Langland, Chaucer, or Spenser describe; they are purely Elizabethan. Lodge could make the Classical contemporary with ease. He had a keen eye for seeing that man's behavior is not new; it only wears different costumes.

As there are seven chief angels, so there are seven chief devils: Leviathan, or pride; Mammon, or avarice; Asmodeus, or lechery; Beelzebub, or envy; Baalberith, or ire; Beelphogor, or gluttony; Astaroth, or sloth. Each of these "incarnate diuels" is listed with his multiple offspring to form a series of character studies. Hence, the Boaster: "Touch me his hat, it was giuen him by Henry the second of Fraunce . . . commend the fashion of his beard, hee tels you it is the worke of a Turkish barber. . . ." [35]

The *miles gloriosus,* the typical braggart familiar in the area of St. Paul's Cathedral like Jonson's Bobadill, is described at length, as is Curiosity in the form of the alchemist, the magician, and the astrologer. Superfluous Invention, or Fashion, is described as follows: "This is he who first found out the inuentions to curle, and to him it is ascribed the changing and dying of haire." [36] Mammon, or avarice, is described as "tormented and waxen old with intollerable desire, finding the world insufficient to satisfie his affections, by cold cathars of iealousie feeling his senses choked, and with a *Paralisis* of feare, shaken almost one ioint from another; betooke himself at last to his caue of suspition, where he suffereth his euidences to be wormeaten for want of opening, and his gold and siluer to rust for want of use." [37] And Lodge's own contemporaries are named as victims of Beelzebub, or envy: "*Lilly*, the famous for facility in discourse: *Spencer*, best read in ancient Poetry: *Daniel*, choise in word, and inuention: *Draiton*, diligent and formall: *Th. Nashe*, true English Aretine." [38]

Under Baalberith's offspring is Brawling Contention, with one of the most colorful descriptions of the English braggart:

Tee first of them became a Ruffian, a Swashbuckler, and a Bragart, they call him *Brawling Contention;* his common gate is as proud as a Spaniards, his ordinary apparell is a little low crownd hat with a fether in it like a forehorse; his haires are curld, and full of elueslocks, and nitty for want of kembing; his eies are still staring, and he neuer lookes on a man but as if he would eate him: his doublet is of cast Satten, cut sometime vpon Taffata, but that the bumbast hath eaten through it, and spotted here and there with pure fat, to testifie that he is a good trencher man: his common course is to go alwaies vntrust, except when his shirt is a washing, & then he goes woolward: and his breeches are as desperate as himselfe, for they are past mending: his weapons are a basket hilted sword, and a bum dagger; and if hee keepe these from pawn, he is sure of a liuing: his praiers in the morning are, Gogs wounds hostesse one pot more: and his daily exercise is to be champion in a bawdy house: you shall haue him for tweluepence to braue and brawle with any man liuing: and let any man fall togither by the eares; to the field (cries hee) Ile see faire play: he hath a Punck (as the Pleasant *Singer* calls her) that finds him spending mony; and if she prouide not his drinking penny, shee is sure of the bastinado: giue him the lie, hee strikes you suddenly; and call him lesse then a gentleman souldier, zownds you are a villaine. He is a passing good railer, specially if an old bawd anger him; and let him but looke into a vawting house, he shall play his tricks without charges. In Terme time he is a Setter, to further horse-stealers; and to cunnycatch a countreman, he shall giue place to none in Newgate. In a fray in

Fleetstreet you shall daily see him foremost, for but in fighting, chiding, and scolding, hee hath no countenance. You shall hire him for a speciall baily if you come off with an angell; and sometimes he may carry a ring in his mouth, if hee haue a cast liuery for his labour. Hee is the only man liuing to bring you where the best licour is, and it is his hat to a halfepenny but hee will be drunke for companie. Then let the host crosse him, out goes his dagger; let the hostesse intreat him, shee is a whore for her labour, and though hee drinke beyond his stocke, thats but a custome. Tut (mine host, cries hee) skore it vp, it is the credit of your alehouse. Bring a Sargeant and him togither, you shall heare villainie with a vengeance: and if they conspire any mans arrest, gogs wounds hee will haulse him. This is a chiefe caterpiller in a citie, and too much winkt at: hee hath alreadie infected the most part of the suburbs, and it were great pittie to graunt him harbour in the citie. . . .[39]

Belphogor, "Prince of Belly-cheere," and Astaroth, or sloth, conclude the pamphlet. Lodge's farewell to the reader is typical of the style he had achieved: balanced, but not artificial, and smooth: "The desire is tedious that hath no end, and the labour loathsome that is misconstrued. You buy that cheape, which cost me deare; and read that with pleasure, which I haue written with trauell: Only if you pay me with the seed of acceptance, you make me forward toward another haruest; and in giuing me thankes, you shall loose nothing." [40]

VII   Teares of Marie

The third pamphlet is openly more Roman Catholic than any other yet published by Lodge: *Prosopopeia, the Teares of the holy, blessed and sanctified Marie, the Mother of God* (1596).[41] For this work, Lodge tells the readers, he read widely in the writings of the Fathers: Bernard, John Damascene, Gregory, Chrysostom, and Augustine, among others: "I haue written nothing without example, I build no waies on mine owne abilitie." [42] The work is dedicated to two most worthy ladies, Margaret Stanley, Countess of Derby, and Margaret Clifford, Countess of Cumberland. The former, Lodge knew from his long connection with the Earls of Derby; the latter was a most devout person with some literary aspirations. Samuel Daniel was a tutor for her daughter, so she was well acquainted with current trends, and is said to have written poems in imitation of Spenser.

Lodge's moral purpose in the *Teares* is clear: "In meditating with Marie, you shall find Iesus: in knowing Christ's sufferance, you shall be inflamed in his loue." [43] The whole is a long discourse of the sufferings of Mary because of the sins rampant in the world and because of man's indifference to his Savior.

The *Teares* is Lodge's last literary production. Since he had announced in it to the world his open acceptance of Roman Catholicism, it is strange that the work was ever printed; but it is not strange that Lodge gave up writing and turned to other pursuits. He was now openly a Roman Catholic, which was dangerous, since Parliament had decreed in 1581 that conversion to Roman Catholicism was treasonable, and he was not content nor successful as a writer. Too many of his epistles to the reader carry a note of dissatisfaction with his career, or with the rewards it had brought. He was not, apparently, interested in law; and he had found no pleasure or profit in his adventures on the seas. England and its customs were closing in on him; he longed for the solitary life so often described in his writings: in the poem "In praise of the Solitarie Life" from *Scillaes Metamorphosis,* and in the recurring figure of the wise hermit, devout, apart, holy, free. Lodge was about to take a step toward this life, but it led in a surprising direction.

CHAPTER 6

A New Road

IN 1597 Lodge began the study of medicine. Now thirty-nine years old, he was no success as a writer, and persecution as a recusant must have followed the publication of his last pamphlets; but to enter a new study and a new way of life at his age was a major step. The reasons for the move are based on conjecture. We know from his past experience that Lodge was anxious to make a firm connection with the spirit of his age, and we know he was leaning more and more to a life of service to mankind. We know as well that he was financially well off after the settlement with William Lodge in 1594. By 1597 he had a house at Low Layton, just outside London. How wealthy he was is not known, but he must have been free of most of his financial problems; for, at the end of 1597, he left England to study medicine at the University at Avignon.

Tenney has pieced together a plausible though conjectural picture of what Lodge found in that ancient city.[1] Avignon, the seat of the Pope during the Catholic schism, had a relatively small faculty of medicine in comparison with other European centers. Lodge may have chosen the school for financial reasons, or for a curriculum that allowed him to complete requirements for the degree in only one year, compared to the usual three. Some of his works indicate he had previously read widely in the theory of medicine.[2]

I Translations

By January, 1598, Lodge had received his degree and had affirmed his strong faith in the Roman religion as he did so.[3] From references in *The Poore Mans Talentt*, we gather that Lodge spent some time practicing medicine in Belgium.[4] He was certainly back in London in 1601, however, for he entered for publication a translation of a work of the eminent Catholic writer Luis of Granada, *The Flowers of Lodowicke of Granada. The First Part . . . translated out of Latine into English by T. L. Doctor of Physicke.* Doctors were to some degree exempt from religious persecution, but Lodge went beyond sense in publishing this translation so soon after his return from the Continent. A number of reasons indicate why the book was allowed: Luis of Granada's works were by no means unknown in England; a host of translations had appeared before Lodge's; furthermore, Luis was not entirely orthodox. The Roman authorities in Spain were not so enthralled with his teachings as were some English readers, for some of his works had been placed on the Index.

In the following year, 1602, Lodge entered another and more extensive translation for publication: Josephus' *The Wars of the Jews.* If he were practicing medicine, he was not overtaxed in this occupation. The translation became a monument to Lodge, a handsome folio edition, entitled *The Famous and Memorable Workes of Iosephus, a Man of Much Honor and Learning Among the Iewes. Faithfully translated out of the Latin, and French, by Tho. Lodge, Doctor in Physic.* Three editions of the work appeared before Lodge's death in 1625, and several editions after that date.

II Treatise of the Plague

The practice of medicine was sufficiently rewarding to encourage Lodge to apply for a similar degree from Oxford; that is, he had his Avignon degree registered at the university, probably for professional reasons. The average Londoner would be more willing to consult a doctor with an English than a Continental degree. The formality was completed in October, 1602.[5] In this same year, he may have written a pamphlet, *Paradoxes against common Opinion.* The work is not signed, but has generally been assigned to Lodge because of the prose style.[6] The attribution is, however, tenuous.

The business of practicing medicine led Lodge to a practical and useful subject. His next work was a medical study based on research into the causes and cures of the plague, *Treatise of the Plague.* The bubonic plague had ravaged England periodically after the great plague of 1348, and Lodge himself lived through two sieges. His experience as an adult and as a physician in the plague of 1603—the year of Elizabeth's death—resulted in his book, which is, in many ways, the crowning achievement of his entire career; for it shows clearly that Lodge was in the role of the "hermit," the wise man who lends his knowledge for the salvation of others. He is now playing the part of Anthony in *The Diuel Coniured.* He is not saving so much men's souls as preserving their bodies from the terrors of the plague: he is the Christian, dedicated doctor, lending the best of his experience for the benefit of mankind.

The work is dedicated to the Lord Mayor and other city officials, whose responsibilities in the time of plague Lodge makes clear in chapters eight and nine.[7] That the treatise is a labor of love is certain from this charge to the mayor: "It resteth in your Honor & those your right worshipfull assistance, to haue especiall care that this charitable intent of mine may be furthered by your discreet orders in such manner that these bookes may be dispearsed among those families that are visited, to the end they may finde comfort and cure by their owne hands and diligence. This is the only reward I require, as Almighty God knoweth, to whose mercy I commend you. From my house in Warwicke Lane, this 19. of August." [8]

One of the most pressing reasons Lodge found it imperative to write the treatise was the presence of charlatans who sought easy money for spurious cures and preventatives: "There haue beene lately certaine *Thessali* that haue bestowed a new Printed liuery on euery olde post, and promised such myracles, as if they were able to make old Aeson young again." [9] One such physician was a neighbor of Lodge's, and his customers sought Lodge in error. Their problems prompted the *Treatise:*

These importunities of theirs made mee both agreeued, and amazed; agreeued, because of that loathsome imposition which was laid vppon me, to make my self vendible (which is vnworthy a liberall & gentle mind, much more ill beseeming a Phisitian and Philosopher, who ought not prostitute so sacred a profession so abiectly, but be a contemner of base and seruile desire of mony . . . amazed, to see the ignorance and error of the multitude, who dare trust their liues to their hands who build their experience on hazard of mens liues.[10]

Some interesting slants are revealed in the epistle: first, Lodge is a humanitarian as never before; the compassion for the ill and for the ignorant is a new note. Secondly, he is now well off: this book was printed at his own expense for distribution to the needy, and he shows a contempt for money not evident a few years previously. Third, he concludes the epistle by defending a particular cure that one of his contemporaries forbids: Dr. Lodge had the stature and the learning and the experience by 1603 to take issue with his fellows.

The *Treatise* is written simply in order to appeal and to be of benefit to a wide range of readers. Lodge begins with the causes of the plague, as understood then: "all pestilential sicknesses, as from the proper cause, are ingendered from the ayre, depraued and altered in his substance, by a certain vicious mixture of corrupted and strange vapours, contrary to the life of man, and corrupting the vitall spirit. . . ." [11]

Much of the pamphlet is devoted to recipes to ward off or cure the plague, recipes gathered from all known sources. Typical is this direction for a Renaissance lozenge:

Take fine Sugar one ounce, of Orace halfe an ounce, of the shell of an Egge the inward skin being taken away halfe an ounce, put the shell of the Egge into Muske Rose water till it be mollified for the space of eight dayes, beat all these to a fine powder, and with Rose water wherein Gum Tracagant hath bene infused, make Pellets according to what bignesse you please. These are very wholesome, and make the breath sweete, and comfort the heart inwardly, and are of a temperate qualitie, which you may keep in your mouth some three houres.[12]

Chapters eight and nine, directed to city officials, urge them to keep the streets clean of sewage and refuse, and to provide for plague victims a hospital where they could be treated properly. In all, the little book is an honest effort to do something about the pestilence, rather than accept its ravages as a matter of bad luck or as a divine visitation due to the sinfulness of the city.

III *On the Continent*

Some time during these years of his early practice (probably 1604), Lodge married the widow of Solomon Aldred, one of the most notorious of Elizabethan spies. Aldred was known to have worked for both the Pope and Queen Elizabeth until his death at Rouen in 1592.[13] His wife, Joan Fernley Aldred, apparently had separated from her husband in 1586, when she was attached to the household of the Countess of Arundel. Philip Howard, the Earl, and his family were known Roman Catholics, and Mrs. Aldred received a pension from Pope Gregory XIII even after Aldred's defection.[14] She seems to have been a pious woman, devoted to her faith.

Doctor Lodge's marriage to Mrs. Aldred, in spite of suggestions of her good character, must have put them under suspicion of the Crown because of her husband's activities and because of her relations with the Howards. This situation probably caused Lodge to fail to receive permission to practice medicine in London. The Royal College of Physicians refused his application, which is understandable, even though Lodge had performed services beyond necessity during the plague: he had scored physicians roundly for deserting London and charging too heavily for their services. These were more than ample reasons for refusing him permission to practice.

By 1605, in fact, affairs were so uncomfortable in London that Lodge returned to Belgium where he had begun practice. He remained on the Continent until 1610, when he again applied for license to practice from the Royal College. Walker and Tenney have found two traces of Lodge in that five-year period, both of which confirm the fact that Lodge was active in the Counter Reformation. Bishop Joseph Hall reports meeting an Englishman, a physician, in Brussels who wished to convert him,[15] and the man could well have been Lodge. The second notice is more certain: The Crown confiscated a letter from a William Jenison to Dr. Lodge, in which there is a reference of mutual acquaintance with Sir William Stanley, a militant Roman Catholic and a traitor to England.[16]

Lodge's activities on the Continent are not clear. He had no settled place of address, and the suggestion is that he moved about the Low Countries and France.[17] From the suggestion in Jenison's letter implying connections with Stanley, it is possible that Lodge and his wife were agents for the Roman Catholic cause. Until more proof is available, however, explanations for Lodge's activities during this period must be only conjecture.

Sometime during 1609, Lodge made overtures to return to England, a return which would not have materialized had not the English ambassador to France, Sir Thomas Edmondes, come to his assistance.[18] With the help of Edmondes, Lodge was not only allowed to reside in London, but admitted to the Royal College of Physicians on March 9, 1610. We do not know exactly what Edmondes did for Lodge, but he acknowledged the favor in a letter to the ambassador: "J haue thought good in these few lines to acknowledg my loue and deuty to your Honnor by whose means J haue not only repossed my Country, but my peace and quietness in the same. To you J ascribe all my good fortunes. . . ."[19] Aside from one or two scrapes with the law over his religion, Lodge lived in relative peace, protected by the ambassador's word to the authorities, and his Oath of Obedience to the Crown, which he swore to in 1611.[20]

IV Last Writings

Lodge was a busy man in the early years of the new century, but he was still somewhat a man of letters. Even though he bade farewell to a literary profession in 1596, as we have seen, several works appeared under his name after that date. Now in 1611 he was ready to present his latest work, a translation of Seneca, *The Workes both Morall and Natural of Lucius Annaeus Seneca*. Certain temporal affairs, however, prevented the work from appearing until 1614. Lodge's brother Nicholas died in 1612 at the family estate at Rolleston, and his death left Lodge executor. His elder brother William had for some reason fled to Ireland; Nicholas left bequests to William and his family, but Lodge fell sole heir to the lands, which must have afforded him some satisfaction after the altercations he had had with William in 1594.[21] With the inheritance, Lodge also inherited a host of lawsuits, some of them old debts of his own. The estate was wealthy, but gave him more than one headache.[22]

The publication of *Seneca* must have eased the pain; a popular work, it went through many editions and has remained a standard English translation. This excerpt from "Of Benefits" illustrates the level of Lodge's prose style in his maturity:

In a word, to the requiting of a good turne there needeth vertue, time, abilitie, and fauourable fortune. Hee that performeth not this (which to atchieue neither requireth labour, nor charge, nor felicitie) hath no couert, or patronage to conceale himselfe in. For neuer meant he to be thankfull, who cast a benefit so farre from him, that it neither suruiued in his sight, nor his remembrance. Euen as those things which are in vse, and are managed and handled daily, are neuer in danger of soile, or rusting; and those which are out of sight, and vse (so as they haue lien by, as vnnecessarie) doe gather soile by continuance of time: So that which frequent cogitation exerciseth and reneweth, is neuer wrought out of memorie, which looseth and forgetteth nothing, but that, which she respecteth and looketh not backe vnto verie often.[23]

Even as he worked on the *Seneca*, Lodge was still a practicing physician. Tenney quotes a letter Lodge wrote to Stephen Powle in 1618, which shows the doctor at work: "The other accident you complaine of is fatnes: and that is eather naturall, or accidental. The naturall, which J coniecture is yours may bee in some sort easied but not eradicated. To ease it is (in a boddie disposed to fatnes), to abstaine from much sleepe, to flie much sittinge. . . ."[24] This advice sounds like that he had given Anne Lodge in *A Fig for Momus*.

By 1620 Lodge was a successful physician, a wealthy landholder, and a renowned translator. He numbered among his friends the English ambassador to France as well as various members of the Howard family, especially Ann Dacres, Countess of Arundel. Though the Howards were well-known Catholics, they were powerful enough to remain immune to persecution. Lodge was involved in a good many other things during these last years, yet he managed to keep his hand in various literary pursuits. In 1620, he prepared a new edition of his *Seneca*, and in 1621, a new work, a translation of Simon Goulart's *Commentaires et Annotations sur la Sepmaine, de la Creation du Monde*, appeared, called *A learned Summary Upon the famous Poeme of William of Saluste, Lord of Bartas*. The

Summary proved to be a popular work, lasting through three editions.

The last writings of Lodge were left in manuscript and were apparently not intended for publication. The Hunterian Club first published the manuscript, *The Poore Mans Talentt*, in 1881. Lodge collected for this work a number of remedies for a number of ailments, much as he had done earlier in the *Treatise of the Plague*. These recipes were intended for his patroness, the Countess of Arundel. There are several chapters giving short diagnoses and cures in *The Poore Mans Talentt*, the last of his works. To "extinguish lusts," one must "Take the worme that shineth by night, drie yt, and giue the poulder thereof." [25]

In the summer of 1625 London was ravaged once more with a plague. In June, Dr. Lodge was appointed plague-surgeon by the Court of Aldermen. He apparently performed his duty well, and lasted through the worst periods of pestilence in the hot summer; but in September he died suddenly and was buried in a mass grave somewhere in London.

V   *Conclusion*

Dr. Lodge left no will, but he left a sort of legacy, as every man does, subject to probate. For the average reader, a few of Lodge's literary productions are worth while: we cannot deny the pleasure of reading certain passages in *Scillaes Metamorphosis*, and we can only praise the fantasy and invention of *Rosalynde*. The wry twists in the satires and epistles of *A Fig for Momus*, the melody and charm of the many lyrics scattered in his works mark him a talented poet. *A Margarite of America* and *Wits Misery* make him an outstanding master of early prose style. It is by the visible bequests we judge first.

And yet there seems more to the story. If he had only written a few pieces, he would hardly deserve more attention than many of his contemporaries. What is more important is the picture of Lodge as a Renaissance man of the ordinary stamp, not a Sir Walter Raleigh, not a Sir Philip Sidney. Thomas Lodge was a man who searched to make a connection with his age as a writer, only to find this connection not worth while; it proved unimportant and full of disillusionment. The Inns of Court, the South Sea voyage, family connections, a literary career—all these were insufficient to produce the bonds which Lodge felt necessary to bring him closer to the world around him. And behind these external gropings for a place was a deeper conflict.

John Donne reflects this same conflict when he wrote, in the 1590's in *Satire III*, a stirring analysis of the young intellectual's search for truth in faith. He came up with no satisfactory answers except that truth stands on a cragged and steep hill, ". . . he that will / Reach her, about must, and about must go." This is Lodge's conflict. He had more of the will to reach than did most of his contemporaries in the "second circle" of Elizabethans.

Two great goals were in his mind: one spiritual, the other temporal. He early in life chose the spiritual goal, and finally achieved it in the craggiest and steepest of places, the Roman faith in Anglican England. Over and over in his works there appears the sense of longing for the contemplative life and for wisdom, whereby he could serve others; a sort of hermit figure to whom the restless could come for guidance. The temporal goal had much the same end: in almost all his writings the wish to teach, to lead men to the good way of life is present. When he failed to achieve that goal as a writer, he turned, at a time when most men refuse to turn, to a new medium of reaching his fellow man: he became a doctor of medicine. While he ministered to the sick, he continued to write as a translator. The list is impressive: *The Flowers of Lodowicke of Granada,* one of the foremost preachers of his day; the *Works* of Josephus on the struggles of the Jews; the philosophical works of Seneca, the great Stoic; and a commentary on DuBartas' *Divine Weeks*. To these we add the *Treatise of the Plague* and *The Poore Mans Talentt,* both arguing a generous and compassionate mind. The tally adds up to a firm connection with his age.

The stars of the Renaissance are Spenser, Shakespeare, Donne, Jonson, and Milton. Lodge, Greene, Nashe, Drayton, Sidney, and Daniel among others played supporting roles. It is traditional to remember Lodge as a writer of lyrics and of prose romance, as the man who gave Shakespeare the material for *As You Like It,* or as one of the foremost translators of Seneca. But his contribution to English letters is much more significant: his prose work gave later writers a style devoid of euphuistic and latinate excess and enriched by tighter plot construction—*Rosalynde* is certainly a forerunner of the modern novel, and *Wits Misery* is an important step toward the English essay. His poetry brought formal satire to English literature in *A Fig for Momus; Scillaes Metamorphosis* opened the way for the Ovidian verse narrative genre; his lyrics contributed the free and graceful expression which marks the best of later poets' work. When we recall that literature was indeed reborn during the English Renaissance, we can see that Lodge contributed much to its birth and its nurture. And, if we add his contributions to humanity as a physician, we must award him a place as one of the most interesting and influential representatives of his age.

Notes and References

CHAPTER ONE

1. Edward Andrews Tenney, *Thomas Lodge* (Ithaca, 1935), p. 70 ff.

2. Charles J. Sisson, "Thomas Lodge and his Family," *Thomas Lodge and Other Elizabethans* (Cambridge, 1933), p. 96.

3. Lawrence A. Sasek, *The Literary Temper of the English Puritans* (Baton Rouge, 1961).

4. *Ibid.*, 95n. Sasek notes that the preface to Philip Stubbe's *Anatomy of the Abuses in England in Shakespeare's Youth A.D. 1583*, ed. F. J. Furnivall (London, 1877), found some good in plays, but this preface was withdrawn in subsequent editions.

5. William Ringler, "The Source of Lodge's Reply to Gosson," *Review of English Studies* XV (1939), 164–71.

6. *Elizabethan Critical Essays*, ed. G. G. Smith (Oxford, 1904), I, 72.

7. *Ibid.*, p. 72.

8. *Ibid.*, p. 83.

9. Stephen Gosson, *The Schoole of Abuse, conteining a pleasunt inuectiue against Poets, Pipers, Plaiers, Iesters, and such like Caterpillers of a Commonwealth . . . ouerthrowing their Bulwarkes, by Prophane Writers, Naturall reason, and common experience . . .* (1579). *Shakespeare Society, Early Treatises on the Stage* (London, 1841).

10. William Ringler, *Stephen Gosson* (Princeton, 1942), p. 48 ff.

11. Gosson, *The Schoole of Abuse, Early Treatises on the Stage,* p. 30.

12. *Ibid.*, p. 25.

13. *Ibid.*, p. 15.

14. *Ibid.*, p. 25.

15. *Ibid.*, p. 24.

16. *Ibid.*, p. 47.

17. One copy is at the Bodleian Library; one at the Huntington Library. Neither copy has a title page. The pamphlet has been

given various titles: *Defense of Poetry, Honest Exuses, Reply to Gosson.* Gosse's reprint of Lodge's *Works* uses the title *Reply to Gosson.*

18. *Reply, Elizabethan Critical Essays,* p. 67.

19. *Ibid.,* p. 68.

20. *Ibid.,* p. 69.

21. *Ibid.,* p. 75.

22. *Ibid.,* p. 76.

23. Gosson, *The Schoole of Abuse, Early Treatises on the Stage,* p. 51.

24. *Reply, Elizabethan Critical Essays,* p. 63.

25. *Ibid.,* p. 64.

26. *Ibid.,* p. 64–72.

27. *The Schoole of Abuse and a Short Apologie for the Schoole of Abuse,* ed. Edward Arber (London, 1895). *A Short Apologie* was originally published as part of Gosson's *Ephemerides of Phialo,* 1579.

28. *A Short Apologie,* p. 73.

29. *Ibid.,* p. 73.

30. Full title: *Playes Confuted in Fiue Actions, prouing that they are not to be suffred in a Christian Common weale, by the waye both the Cauils of Thomas Lodge, and the Play of Playes, written in their defense, and other obiections of Players frendes, are truely set downe and directlye aunsweared.* ed. W. C. Hazlitt, Roxburghe Library (London, 1869), pp. 157–66.

31. *Playes Confuted* (Hazlitt), p. 160.

32. *Ibid.*

33. *Ibid.,* p. 169.

34. *Ibid.,* p. 171.

35. Tenney, p. 79.

36. This might not be our Thomas Lodge, as Alice Walker suggests in *RES* IX (1933), 427, 429.

37. Tenney, p. 80.

38. *The Work of Thomas Lodge,* ed. Sir Edmund Gosse (Glasgow, 1875–88), IV, "Miscellaneous Pieces."

CHAPTER TWO

1. Sisson gives extensive background on the Lodge lawsuits in Chapter III, "Thomas Lodge and his Brothers," pp. 80–117.

2. N. Burton Paradise, *Thomas Lodge, The History of an Elizabethan* (New Haven, 1931), p. 24.

3. Sisson, pp. 155–56.

4. *Works,* I, 7.

5. *Ibid.*, p. 8.
6. *Ibid.*, p. 5.
7. *Ibid.*, p. 9.
8. *Ibid.*
9. See note 1 directly above.
10. *Works*, I, 13.
11. *Ibid.*, p. 14.
12. *Ibid.*
13. *Ibid.*, p. 22.
14. *Ibid.*, p. 28.
15. *Ibid.*, p. 41.
16. *Ibid.*, p. 42.
17. *Ibid.*, p. 43.
18. *Ibid.*, p. 51.
19. *Forbonius and Prisceria, Works,* I, 59.
20. *Ibid.*, p. 56.
21. *Ibid.*, p. 84.
22. *Ibid.*, p. 56.
23. *Ibid.*, p. 57.
24. *Ibid.*, p. 56.
25. *Ibid.*, p. 57.
26. Paradise, p. 78.
27. *Ibid.*
28. *Truth's Complaint, Works,* I, 87.
29. Paradise, p. 36.
30. *Ibid.*, p. 37.
31. Tenney, pp. 96–97.
32. Pat M. Ryan, Jr., *Thomas Lodge, Gentleman* (Hamden, Conn., 1958), 76–77.
33. Paradise, pp. 129–37. See note 4, p. 129, for history of the date controversy.
34. Full title: *An Auncient Historie and exquisite Chronicle of the Romanes warres, both Ciuile and Foren. Written in Greeke by the noble Orator and Historiographer, Appian of Alexandria, one of the learned Counsell to the most mightie Emperoures, Traiane and Adriane.*
35. Paradise, pp. 137–41. J. D. Wilson first suggested the source in an edition of *Wounds* for the Malone Society (Oxford, 1910), Introduction, p. xii.
36. *Wounds of Ciuil War,* Works, III, 4. Subsequent references are listed in the text.
37. Paradise, p. 152, suggests 1587. Tenney, p. 99, does not suggest a date.

38. *Henslowe's Diary*, ed. W. W. Greg (London, 1904), I, 13–15.
39. *A Looking Glass for London and England*, ed. W. W. Greg (Oxford, 1932), Introduction, pp. vi–vii.
40. *A Looking Glass for London and England, Works*, IV.

CHAPTER THREE

1. Full title: *Scillaes Metamorphosis: Enterlaced with the vnfortunate loue of Glaucus. VVhereunto is annexed the delectable discourse of the discontented Satyre: with Sundrie other most absolute Poems and Sonnets. Containing the destestable tyrannie of Disdaine, and Comicall triumph of Constancie: Verie fit for young Courtiers to peruse and coy Dames to remember. Works*, I.
2. Douglas Bush, *Mythology and the Renaissance Tradition* (New York, 1957), Chapter IV, pp. 68–85.
3. *Ibid.*, pp. 70–71.
4. Hallett Smith, *Elizabethan Poetry* (Cambridge, 1952), pp. 68–75.
5. *Ibid.*, p. 73.
6. Works, I, 4.
7. *Tudor Poetry and Prose*, ed. J. William Hebel, Hoyt H. Hudson, *et. al.* (New York, 1953), pp. 39–40.
8. *Ars Poetica* (Cambridge, 1961), ll. 148–50.
9. Smith, *Elizabethan Poetry*, p. 76.
10. *Ibid.*
11. Bush, p. 81.
12. Paradise, p. 82.
13. *Ibid.*, p. 83.
14. John Peter, *Complaint and Satire in Early English Literature* (Oxford, 1956), p. 136.
15. *Discontented Satyre, Works*, I, 31.
16. L. E. Kastner, *Athenaeum*, Oct. 22, 1904, p. 552.
17. *Works*, I, 37.
18. *Ibid.*, p. 39.
19. Paradise, p. 82.
20. *Ibid.*, p. 85.
21. *Works*, I, 46.
22. *The Poems of Sir Walter Ralegh*, ed. Agnes Latham (London, 1951), p. 11.
23. *Works*, I, 43.
24. Kastner, *Athenaeum*, Oct. 22, 1904, p. 552.
25. *Works*, I, 47–48.
26. *Rosalynde, Works*, I, 4.
27. *Ibid.*

28. *Ibid.*, p. 8.
29. Paradise, p. 87.
30. Wilbur L. Cross, *The Development of the English Novel* (London, 1913), p. 13.
31. *Memoir, Works*, I, 21.
32. J. J. Jusserand, *The English Novel in the Time of Shakespeare*, transl. Elizabeth Lee (London, 1908), pp. 213–14.
33. *Tudor Poetry and Prose* contains several, pp. 156–57. *The Renaissance in England*, ed. Hyder E. Rollins and Herschel Baker (Boston, 1954), p. 763 ff.
34. *Works*, I, 29–30.
35. *Ibid.*, p. 49.
36. *Ibid.*, p. 102.
37. *Ibid.*, p. 118.
38. *Ibid.*, p. 137.
39. *Ibid.*, p. 136.
40. *Ibid.*, p. 40.
41. *Ibid.*, p. 79.
42. Paradise, p. 91.
43. Walter Raleigh, *The English Novel* (London, 1904), p. 70.
44. See Paradise's discussion, pp. 87–91.
45. *Rosalynde, Works*, I, 9.
46. *Ibid.*, p. 10.
47. *Ibid.*, p. 11.
48. *Ibid.*, pp. 16–17.
49. *Ibid.*, p. 37.
50. *Ibid.*, p. 81.
51. *Ibid.*, p. 139.

CHAPTER FOUR

1. *Robert Duke of Normandy, Works*, II, 3.
2. *Ibid.*, p. 9.
3. *Ibid.*, p. 40.
4. *Ibid.*, pp. 41–42.
5. *Catharos, Works*, II, 3.
6. *Ibid.*, p. 8.
7. *Ibid.*, pp. 24–25.
8. *Euphues Shadow, Works*, II, 9.
9. C. S. Lewis, *English Literature in the Sixteenth Century* (Oxford, 1954), pp. 489–90.
10. *Euphues Shadow, Works*, II, 25.
11. *Ibid.*, p. 28.
12. *Ibid.*, p. 92.

13. *Ibid.,* p. 9.
14. *Ibid.,* p. 16.
15. Tenney, p. 111.
16. *Ibid.,* pp. 109–10.
17. *Euphues Shadow, Works,* II, 104.
18. Tenney, Chap. VI, p. 114 ff.
19. *A Margarite of America, Works,* III, 3.
20. Tenney, pp. 111–12.
21. Sisson, pp. 89–100.
22. *William Longbeard, Works,* II, 4.
23. Tenney, p. 130.
24. Paradise, p. 43.
25. *Ibid.,* p. 102.
26. See L. E. Kastner, *Athenaeum,* Oct. 22, 1904, pp. 552–53, and Oct. 29, 1904, p. 591. Also his article in *Modern Language Review,* "Thomas Lodge as an Imitator of the Italian Poets," II (1907), pp. 155–61. Alice Walker, "Italian Sources for Lyrics of Thomas Lodge," *Modern Language Review,* XXII (1927), pp. 75–79. Marion Grubb, "Lodge's Borrowings from Ronsard," *Modern Language Notes,* XLV (1930), pp. 357–60.
27. *Phillis, Works,* II, 4.
28. *Ibid.,* p. 5.
29. *Ibid.,* p. 6.
30. *Ibid.*
31. *Ibid.,* p. 19.
32. *Ibid.,* p. 54.
33. *Ibid.,* p. 9.
34. *Ibid.,* p. 17.
35. *Ibid.,* p. 40.
36. *English Literature in the Sixteenth Century,* pp. 494–95.
37. *Phillis, Works,* II, 50, 51.
38. *Ibid.,* p. 35.
39. *Ibid.,* p. 58.
40. *Miscellaneous Pieces, Works,* IV, 6–7.
41. *Ibid.,* p. 16.
42. *Ibid.,* pp. 17–18.
43. *Ibid.,* p. 19.
44. *Ibid.,* pp. 20–21.

CHAPTER FIVE

1. *A Fig for Momus, Works,* III, 5.
2. *Ibid.,* p. 6.

3. *Ibid.*, pp. 6–7.

4. *Ibid.*, p. 11. Satire 1 is dedicated to "E. Dig." Tenney (p. 145) believes the man is an E. Digby, Master of the Revels at Lincoln's Inn in 1572, or Everard Digby, author of several treatises in 1578–1579.

5. In numbering the Satires, Lodge omits number 2. Satire 3 is the second.

6. *Works*, III, 35.

7. *Juvenal and Persius*, transl. G. G. Ramsay (London, 1957), XIV, ll. 31–41.

8. *Works*, III, 48.

9. *Juvenal and Persius*, X, ll. 1–4.

10. *Satires, Epistles and Ars Poetica*, transl. H. Rushton Fairclough (London, 1961), II, vi, ll. 1–4.

11. *Works*, III, 44–45.

12. Epistle 2 is dedicated to "Master W. Bolton." C. S. Lewis mentions an Edmund Bolton (1575?–1633?), not in connection with Lodge, who contributed the "Palinode" in *England's Helicon* (*English Literature in the Sixteenth Century* [522]), but there is no reason to believe he can be indentified with Lodge's Bolton.

13. Henri Cornelius Agrippa, *Of the Vanitie and Uncertaintie of the Artes and Sciences* (London, 1569). Edgar Hill Duncan noted Lodge's reliance on Agrippa, "Thomas Lodge's Use of Agrippa's Chapter on Alchemy," *Vanderbilt Studies in the Humanities*, I (1951), 96–105.

14. J. W. Lever, *Elizabethan Love Sonnet* (London, 1956), wrongly calls "A. L." Lodge's wife.

15. *Works*, III, 52 ff. The epistle is wrongly numbered "6" in the *Works*.

16. Tenney, pp. 52–53.

17. *Works*, III, 14.

18. *Ibid.*, p. 60.

19. *Works*, ed. A. H. Bullen (London, 1887) III, viii, ll. 122–25.

20. *Works*, ed. J. William Hebel (Oxford, 1961), I, ll. 1001–4.

21. *Greek Bucolic Poets*, transl. J. M. Edmonds (London, 1938), XVI, 189.

22. *Pastoral Poetry and Pastoral Drama* (London, 1906), p. 113.

23. *Memoir, Works*, I, 39.

24. Ernest A. Baker, *The History of the English Novel*, II, "The Elizabethan Age and After" (New York, 1929), p. 119.

25. *English Literature in the Sixteenth Century*, p. 424.

26. *Ibid.*, p. 425.

27. *A Margarite of America, Works,* III, 3.

28. John Garrett Underhill, *Spanish Influence in the England of the Tudors* (New York, 1899), p. 312.

29. *Works,* III, 4.

30. *Ibid.*

31. *Ibid.,* p. 11.

32. *Memoir, Works,* I, 40.

33. *The Diuel Coniured, Works,* III, 3.

34. *Ibid.,* p. 13.

35. *Wits Misery, Works,* IV, 10.

36. *Ibid.,* p. 19.

37. *Ibid.,* p. 32.

38. *Ibid.,* p. 63.

39. *Ibid.,* pp. 68–69.

40. *Ibid.,* p. 117.

41. The epistle to the readers is signed *L. T.* See Paradise, p. 126.

42. *Prosopopeia, Works,* III, 12.

43. *Ibid.,* p. 12.

CHAPTER SIX

1. Tenney, Chap. VIII, p. 155 ff.

2. *A Fig for Momus,* Epistles, 2, 3; *Wits Misery,* p. 79 *passim.*

3. Tenney, pp. 160–62.

4. *Works,* IV.

5. Tenney, pp. 165–66.

6. Paradise, pp. 166–67.

7. *A Treatise of the Plague: containing the nature, signes and accidents of the same, with the certaine and absolute cure of the Feuers, Botches and Carbuncles that raigne in these times: And aboue all things most singular Experiments and preseruatiues in the same, gathered by the observation of diuers worthy Trauailers, and selected out of the writings of the best learned Phisitians in this age. Works,* IV.

8. *Ibid.,* p. 4.

9. *Ibid.,* p. 5.

10. *Ibid.,* pp. 5–6.

11. *Ibid.,* p. 14.

12. *Ibid.,* p. 30.

13. Tenney, p. 172.

14. *Ibid.*

15. *Ibid.,* p. 174; Alice Walker, *Review of English Studies,* X, 47–48.

16. Tenney, p. 176.

17. *Ibid.*, pp. 176–77.

18. See Joseph W. Houppert, "Thomas Lodge's Letters to William Trumbull," *Renaissance News*, XVIII (Summer, 1965), 117–123, which reports the discovery of letters helping to date Lodge's exiles on the Continent.

19. Quoted in Tenney, p. 178, from W. W. Greg, *English Literary Autographs, 1550–1650* (Oxford, 1925), I, XIX.

20. The oath is quoted in full, Tenney, p. 179.

21. Sisson thinks he fled because of unwise land speculation, p. 129.

22. Tenney, p. 184; Sisson, p. 132 ff.

23. *Seneca* (London, 1620), Book III, Chap. II.

24. Letter quoted in full, Paradise, pp. 61–62.

25. *Works*, IV, 81.

Selected Bibliography

Primary Sources

LODGE, THOMAS. *The Complete Works of Thomas Lodge.* Ed. Sir Edmund Gosse. 4 vols. Edinburgh: The Hunterian Society, 1875–88. In 1963, Russell and Russell, Inc., reissued the Hunterian Society edition.

Translations

The Famous and Memorable Workes of Josephus. . . . Faithfully translated out of the Latin, and French, by Tho. Lodge Doctor in Physicke. London: Printed at the charges of G. Bishop, S. Waterson, P. Short, and Tho. Adams, 1602.

The Flowers of Lodowicke of Granada. . . . Translated out of Latine into Englishe by T. L. Doctor of Physicke. London: J. Roberts for T. Hayes, 1601.

A Learned Summary upon the Famous Poeme of William of Saluste Lorde of Bartas. . . . Translated out of French, by T. L. D. M. P. London: John Grismand, 1621.

The Workes both Morrall and Natural of Lucius Annaeus Seneca. Translated by T. Lodge D. of Phis. London: William Stansby, 1614.

Secondary Sources

ALDEN, R. M. *The Rise of Formal Satire in England.* Philadelphia: The University Press, 1899. Although somewhat dated, this is a complete history of the genre in English literature, with attention to Classical and Continental influences.

BAKER, ERNEST A. *The History of the English Novel.* Vol. II. New York: Barnes and Noble, 1929. The beginnings of prose fiction in the Elizabethan Age.

BUSH, DOUGLAS. *Mythology and the Renaissance Tradition.* New York: Pageant Book Company, 1957. The influence of Classical myths on major and minor Renaissance writers.

CROSS, WILBUR. *The Development of the English Novel.* London:

Macmillan and Company, 1913. Early chapters discuss the rise of prose fiction in the Elizabethan Age.

DUNCAN, EDGAR HILL. "Thomas Lodge's Use of Agrippa's Chapter on Alchemy," *Vanderbilt Studies in the Humanities*, Vol. I (1951), 96–105. The background for Lodge's Epistle Seven of *A Fig for Momus*.

FREEDMAN, LILA HERRMAN. "Satiric Personae: A Study of Point of View in Formal Verse Satire in the English Renaissance from Wyatt to Marston." University of Wisconsin Doctoral Dissertation, 1956. A detailed study of purpose in satires of Renaissance writers.

GREG, W. W., ed. *Henslowe's Diary*. 2 Vols. Oxford: The University Press, 1904, 1908. Invaluable records of a theater manager in the Elizabethan Age.

————. *Pastoral Poetry and Pastoral Drama*. New York: Russell and Russell, 1959. A study of the pastoral tradition and its influence on Renaissance poets and playwrights.

GRUBB, MARION. "Lodge's Borrowings from Ronsard," *Modern Language Notes*, XLV (1930), 357–60. Traces the influence of Ronsard on Lodge's lyrics, especially in *Phillis*.

JUSSERAND, J. J. *The English Novel in the Time of Shakespeare*. Transl. Elizabeth Lee. London: T. F. Unwin, 1908. Discusses English prose fiction as it arose from various sources in the Renaissance.

KASTNER, L. E. *Athenaeum*. October 22, 1904, pp. 552–53; October 29, 1904, p. 591. Discusses Lodge's borrowings from the writers of the *Pleiade*.

————. "Thomas Lodge as an Imitator of the Italian Poets," *Modern Language Review* XXII (1927), 75–79. Influence of Italian Renaissance poets on Lodge's lyrics.

LEVER, J. W. *The Elizabethan Love Sonnet*. London: Methuen, 1956. The history of the Petrarchan sonnet sequences as they developed in England.

LEWIS, C. S. *English Literature in the Sixteenth Century*. Oxford: The University Press, 1954. Invaluable study of Renaissance literature.

McALEER, JOHN J. "Thomas Lodge's Verse Interludes," *College Language Association Journal*, VI (1962), 83–89. Study of the verse Lodge wrote for the prose romances.

PARADISE, N. BURTON. *Thomas Lodge, The History of an Elizabethan*. New Haven: Yale University Press, 1931. Earliest of modern studies of Lodge's life and works.

PETER, JOHN. *Complaint and Satire in Early English Literature*.

Oxford: The Clarendon Press, 1956. A clear definition of these genres; also a comprehensive study of their development in English literature.

RALEGH, SIR WALTER. *The Poems of Sir Walter Ralegh*. Ed. Agnes Latham. London: Routledge and Paul, 1951. Modern edition of Ralegh's poetry, with a helpful introduction.

RALEIGH, SIR WALTER A. *The English Novel*. London: J. Murray, 1904. Early history of the development of prose fiction in England.

RINGLER, WILLIAM. *Stephen Gosson*. Princeton: Princeton University Press, 1942. Biography of Gosson and critical comment on the stage controversy.

——————. "The Source of Lodge's Reply to Gosson," *Review of English Studies* XV (1939), 164–77. Lodge's indebtedness to Continental writers for the *Reply*.

RYAN, PAT M., JR. *Thomas Lodge, Gentleman*. Hamden, Conn.: The Shoestring Press, 1958. General study of Lodge's life and works; not a scholarly work.

SASEK, LAURENCE A. *The Literary Temper of the English Puritans*. Baton Rouge: Louisiana State University Press, 1961. Discusses the stage controversy and Puritan opposition to entertainment in general.

SISSON, CHARLES. *Thomas Lodge and Other Elizabethans*. Cambridge: Harvard University Press, 1933. Detailed biographical account of Lodge's life.

SMITH, GREGORY. *Elizabethan Critical Essays*. Oxford: The University Press, 1904. The introduction is an excellent study of Elizabethan critical theory, and includes a section on the stage controversy. A portion of Lodge's *Reply* is reprinted.

SMITH, HALLETT. *Elizabethan Poetry*. Cambridge: Harvard University Press, 1952. Critical study of various genres of Elizabethan poetry, including Ovidian verse narrative and the sonnet sequences.

SORENSEN, KNUD. "Thomas Lodge's Seneca," *Archiv für das Studien der neueren Sprachen und Literaturen* (December, 1962), pp. 313–24. Discusses style and other achievements of Lodge's translation.

TANNENBAUM, SAMUEL A. *Thomas Lodge: A Concise Bibliography*. New York: S. A. Tannenbaum, 1940. Invaluable collection of Lodge works and critical studies on them, through 1940.

TENNEY, EDWARD A. *Thomas Lodge*. Ithaca: Cornell University Press, 1935. A scholar's careful study of Lodge's biography and works.

WALKER, ALICE. "Italian Sources for Lyrics of Thomas Lodge," *Modern Language Review* XXII (1927), 75–79. Influence of Italian Renaissance poets on Lodge's lyrics.

——————. "Life of Thomas Lodge," *Review of English Studies* IX (1933), 410–32; X (1934), 46–54. The two articles cover the biography of Lodge and his family.

——————. "Some Sources of the Prose Pamphlets of Thomas Lodge," *Review of English Studies* VIII (1932), 264–81. Discusses possible sources for *Wits Misery, The Diuel Coniured,* and other prose works.

Index